KT-375-957

Owner's Question & Answer Book

Bradley Viner

Photographs by Jane Burton

BLANDFORD

A QUARTO BOOK

Copyright © 1998 Quarto plc

First published in the UK 1999 by
Blandford

A Cassell imprint

Cassell plc,
Wellington House
125 Strand
London WC2R 0BB

www.cassell.co.uk

All rights reserved. No part of this book may be reproduced
in any form, by photostat, microfilm, xerography, or by any
other means, or incorporated into any information retrieval
system, electronic or mechanical, without the written
permission of the copyright owner.

A Cataloguing-in-Publication Data entry for this title is
available and may be obtained from the British Library

ISBN 0-7137-2770-5

Designed and produced by
Quarto Publishing plc,
The Old Brewery, 6 Blundell Street,
London N7 9BH

Project editor: **Anne Hildyard**
Art editor: **Michelle Stamp**
Copy editor: **Eleanor van Zandt**
Picture researcher: **Gill Metcalfe**
Art director: **Moira Clinch**
Index: **Dawn Butcher**

Typeset by Central Southern Typesetters, Eastbourne, UK
Manufactured in Singapore by United Graphics (Pte) Ltd.
Printed in Singapore by Star Standard Industries (Pte) Ltd.

About this Book

The cat holds a unique place in our society. Originally kept to control the rodent population, it has been both revered and persecuted, but has now overtaken the dog as the number one pet in the United Kingdom. This is because the cat fits in so well with our modern lifestyle. Able to form an affectionate relationship with its owners, it maintains the independence that allows it to roam freely and fend for itself.

Cats also fit into a more crowded urban or suburban environment with less problems than other pets, such as dogs. Of course, a very high density of domestic cats in an area can be a nuisance, but cats are not noisy, are very rarely aggressive to people, and usually bury their faeces in areas that do not inconvenience people. Although the role of the cat as rodent control officer is now much less important, their role as stressbuster is becoming stronger. Scientific evidence points to the physical and mental benefits that we gain from having a pet as a companion and high blood pressure and high blood cholesterol levels are significantly lower amongst pet owners. It is also essential that potential cat owners appreciate the time, resources and commitment needed to care for the animal during the whole of its life. The questions in this book focus on basic problems facing cat owners regarding the health or welfare of their pets. To help you find the topics you require, there are three aids in the book: the contents, where all 300 questions are listed; the solution finders, which feature important questions with diagnostic charts that show the possible causes of symptoms and their likely solutions; and the index, which separates the subjects alphabetically.

contents

solution finder

HOW CAN I PROTECT MY CAT'S HEALTH AND WELFARE?

ARE YOU WORRIED ABOUT YOUR CAT HAVING AN ACCIDENT OR INJURY? → YES

DO THE OTHER CATS IN THE NEIGHBOURHOOD POSE A PROBLEM? — YES / NO — **ARE YOU AFRAID OF LOSING YOUR CAT?**

YES / NO / YES / NO

SPAYING OR NEUTERING MAY ALLEVIATE THE PROBLEM; HAVE YOUR CAT VACCINATED.

ACCIDENTS ARE MORE LIKELY IN URBAN AREAS. FIND OUT WHAT TO DO IN AN EMERGENCY.

ENSURE THAT YOUR CAT IS IDENTIFIABLE AND TAKE CARE IF TRAVELLING WITH YOUR CAT.

INDOOR CATS NEED PLENTY TO OCCUPY THEM. ALWAYS OBSERVE BASIC HYGIENE RULES.

ARE YOU CONCERNED ABOUT YOUR CAT'S ENVIRONMENT?

NO

DO YOU WANT TO BREED OR SHOW YOUR CAT?

ARE YOU WORRIED ABOUT HEALTH PROBLEMS RELATED TO BREEDING OR SHOWING?

YES   NO

ARE YOU WORRIED ABOUT LEAVING YOUR CAT ALONE?

YES   NO   YES   NO

BE AWARE OF ANY POSSIBLE PROBLEMS THAT MAY ARISE.

KNOW WHAT TO EXPECT FOR BOTH YOU AND YOUR CAT.

MOST CATS ARE INDEPENDENT. WITH PLANNING, THERE SHOULD BE NO PROBLEMS.

TO KEEP YOUR CAT HAPPY AND HEALTHY, GIVE IT PLENTY OF CARE AND ATTENTION.

I AM HAVING PROBLEMS WITH MY CAT'S ELIMINATION HABITS.

IS YOUR CAT SOILING AROUND THE HOME?

YES

DOES IT APPEAR TO BE INTENTIONAL BEHAVIOUR?

YES   **NO**

DOES YOUR CAT REFUSE TO GO OUTSIDE?

YES   **NO**   **YES**   **NO**

YOUR CAT MAY BE FEELING VULNERABLE, OR IT MAY BE TERRITORY MARKING.

SEE:
40 How do I get my cat to use the litter tray?
41 How can I train my cat to relieve itself outdoors?
44 Should I get a cat flap?
143 Why do cats bury their faeces?
144 How can I stop my cat from spraying urine around the house?
144 My neutered male cat urinates and defecates in corners. What can I do about it?

YOU MAY NEED TO CHANGE THE TYPE OF LITTER OR TRAIN YOUR CAT TO GO OUTSIDE.

SEE:
40 How do I get my cat to use the litter tray?
41 When my cat urinates he sprays so high, it goes over the edge of the litter tray. What is the answer?
41 How can I train my cat to relieve itself outdoors?
44 Should I get a cat flap?

THIS COULD BE NERVOUS BEHAVIOUR.

SEE:
41 How can I train my cat to relieve itself outdoors?
44 My new house already has a cat flap, but my stupid cat won't use it!
144 My nine-month-old male cat goes out but rushes back to use his litter. Should I take it away?

THERE IS NO PROBLEM UNLESS YOUR CAT IS SOILING SOMEONE ELSE'S PROPERTY.

SEE:
143 My neighbour gets very upset about my cats messing on her lawn. Is there anything I can do?
143 Why do cats bury their faeces?

IS THIS A HOUSE TRAINING PROBLEM?

IS THIS A URINARY PROBLEM?

NO

IS YOUR CAT STRAINING TO URINATE?

YES **NO**

IS YOUR CAT STRAINING TO DEFECATE?

YES

NO

YES

NO

THERE MAY BE A BLOCKAGE THAT NEEDS URGENT TREATMENT.

THIS IS LIKELY TO BE AN INFECTION OR A DIETARY PROBLEM.

YOUR CAT IS PROBABLY CONSTIPATED.

DIARRHOEA CAN BE A SIGN OF SERIOUS ILLNESS OR DIETARY PROBLEMS.

SEE:
103 How can I tell if my cat needs immediate veterinary attention?
109 Should I panic if my cat is straining to urinate or defecate?

SEE:
61 Is it OK to give a cat only dry food?
63 My vet says that a special diet can dissolve bladder stones. Can this be true?
90 My cat keeps getting cystitis, despite being fed a special diet. What more can I do?
99 How on earth can I collect a urine sample for testing from my cat?

SEE:
59 How can I prevent my cat from getting constipated?
69 Will grooming prevent my cat from getting hairballs?
109 Should I panic if my cat is straining to urinate or defecate?

SEE:
51 What should I do if my kitten becomes ill?
62 Should I give my cat milk to drink?
82 How will I know when my cat is ill?
83 What does it mean if my cat's third eyelids protrude over part of the eye?
97 What is inflammatory bowel disease?
103 How can I tell if my cat needs immediate veterinary attention?

I AM CONCERNED ABOUT MY CAT'S EATING HABITS.

IS YOUR CAT GAINING WEIGHT?

YES

COULD YOUR CAT BE PREGNANT?

YES   **NO**

IS YOUR CAT LOSING WEIGHT OR SHOWING SIGNS OF OTHER PROBLEMS?

YES

NO

YES

NO

SHE MAY NEED A SPECIAL DIET AND FURTHER CARE FOR HER AND HER KITTENS.

YOU MAY BE OVERFEEDING YOUR CAT.

YOUR CAT MAY BE SICK OR ALLERGIC TO ITS DIET.

YOUR CAT IS PROBABLY HEALTHY.

SEE:
116 How can I tell if my cat is pregnant?
117 How should I feed my cat during her pregnancy?
122 What can I do if my cat cannot or will not feed her kittens?
124 How do I wean kittens onto solid food?

SEE:
57 How often should I feed my cat?
57 How can I tell if my cat is overweight?
58 Is it harmful for a cat to be overweight?
58 How can I get some weight off my rather tubby cat?
64 What is the best diet for my diabetic cat?
81 How can I weigh my cat?

SEE:
53 What extra care does an elderly cat need?
59 How can I prevent my cat from getting constipated?
62 Are there any cat foods that can be harmful to my cat?
62 Should I give my cat milk to drink?
63 My cat keeps getting skin problems. It it possible that she is allergic to something in her diet?
64 My cat is very prone to vomiting. What diet is best for her?
65 Are there any special dietary needs for elderly cats?
65 My elderly cat now eats a lot more food but is losing weight. Is this because of worms?
85 My 15-year-old cat is drinking a lot. Should I be concerned?

SEE:
57 How often should I feed my cat?
59 How can I encourage my kitten to drink more?
60 Why do cats eat grass?
60 My cat chews on houseplants. Can this be dangerous?
61 Are fresh meat and fish best for cats?
61 Can I feed my cat on a vegetarian diet?
61 Is it OK to give a cat only dry food?
62 Are there any cat foods that can be harmful to my cat?
62 I feed my cat on tinned food. Should I also give a vitamin and mineral supplement?

IS YOUR CAT EATING AND DRINKING REGULARLY?

IS YOUR CAT LOSING WEIGHT?

NO

IS YOUR CAT EATING
AND DRINKING
ANYTHING?

YES

NO

DOES YOUR CAT HAVE
ANY OTHER PROBLEMS?

YES

NO

YES

NO

**YOUR CAT MAY
BE SICK OR HAVE
DIFFICULTY
EATING.**

**YOUR CAT IS
PROBABLY VERY
SICK.**

**YOUR CAT MAY
NOT BE GETTING
PROPER
NUTRITION.**

**YOUR CAT MAY
BE EATING
ELSEWHERE.**

SEE:
53 What extra care does an
elderly cat need?
64 My cat has had several
teeth removed. Will she
be able eat her food?
64 Should I worry if my cat
doesn't eat for a day or
two?
65 Are there any special
dietary needs for elderly
cats?
65 My cat has a special diet
for kidney disease. How
can I get him to realise
that he has to eat it?

SEE:
81 How can I weigh my cat?
81 How long can a cat
survive without eating?
82 How will I know when my
cat is ill?
98 How can you nourish a
sick cat that refuses to
take food or water?
98 How can I force-feed my
sick cat?

SEE:
53 What extra care does an
elderly cat need?
59 How can I prevent my cat
from getting constipated?
62 Are there any cat foods
that can be harmful to
my cat?
62 Should I give my cat milk
to drink?
64 My cat is prone to
vomiting. What diet is
best for her?
65 Are there any special
dietary needs for elderly
cats?
134 My cat loves to suck on
wool, and even bites
chunks out of my
sweater. Why does he do
this? Can it be harmful?

SEE:
53 My two 13-year-old cats
now live with my
neighbour, who feeds
them all the time. What
can I do?
62 My cat likes eating dog
food with my dog. Should
this be happening?
64 Should I worry if my cat
doesn't eat for a day or
two?

I AM CONCERNED ABOUT MY CAT'S COAT.

IS YOUR CAT'S COAT IN POOR CONDITION?

DOES YOUR CAT HAVE ANY LESIONS OR SKIN IRRITATION?

YES   **NO**

DO YOU GROOM YOUR CAT REGULARLY?

YES   **NO**   **YES**   **NO**

THIS COULD BE A REACTION TO DIET, TO PARASITES OR EXPOSURE TO THE SUN.

THIS COULD BE DUE TO OLD AGE OR YOUR CAT MAY BE SICK.

SOME CATS NEED LESS GROOMING THAN OTHERS.

REGULAR GROOMING WILL PREVENT A LOT OF PROBLEMS.

MY CAT KEEPS VOMITING. WHY IS THIS?

COULD YOUR CAT HAVE EATEN SOMETHING TO UPSET IT?

COULD THIS HAVE BEEN A PLANT?		DOES YOUR CAT VOMIT REGULARLY?
	YES NO	
YES	NO YES	NO

YOUR CAT MAY HAVE EATEN GRASS OR A POISONOUS PLANT.

YOUR CAT MAY HAVE SWALLOWED A FOREIGN BODY.

THIS COULD BE A DIGESTIVE PROBLEM OR A SIGN OF SERIOUS ILLNESS.

THIS IS PROBABLY A NERVOUS BEHAVIOURAL PROBLEM.

SEE:
60 Why do cats eat grass?
60 My cat chews on houseplants. Can this be dangerous?
87 What are the common causes of poisoning in the cat?

SEE:
43 Can some toys be harmful?
69 Will grooming keep my cat from getting hairballs?
109 How can I help my cat if he seems to be choking?
134 My cat loves to suck on wool, and even bites chunks out of my sweater. Why does he do this, and can it be harmful?

SEE:
51 What should I do if my kitten becomes ill?
64 My cat is prone to vomiting. What diet is best for her?
82 How will I know when my cat is ill?
83 My cat vomits quite regularly. Is this normal?
97 What is inflammatory bowel disease?
103 How can I tell if my cat needs immediate veterinary attention?

SEE:
149 My cat often vomits in the living room, especially when I have guests. Why is this?
157 My cat throws up in the car on the way to cat shows and never wins because he gets all dirty!

I AM CONCERNED ABOUT MY CAT'S BEHAVIOUR.

IS THE BEHAVIOUR AGGRESSIVE?

YES

IS THE BEHAVIOUR IN RESPONSE TO HANDLING?

YES   NO

IS THE BEHAVIOUR VOCAL?

YES   NO

YES   NO   YES   NO

YOUR CAT NEEDS SOCIALIZING OR IS NOT ACCUSTOMED TO THE WAY IT IS BEING HANDLED.

THIS MAY BE TERRITORIAL BEHAVIOUR.

YOUR CAT IS PROBABLY A VOCAL BREED, MAY BE IN SEASON, OR IS JUST TALKING TO YOU.

THIS SOUNDS LIKE NORMAL CAT BEHAVIOUR.

SEE:
51 What is the correct way to pick up a kitten?
69 My cat gets really aggressive when I try to groom him. How can I cope?
123 How soon should I handle my new kittens?
139 What does it mean when a cat wags its tail?
145 I can't cuddle my kitten. She twists and scratches until I put her down. Will I ever be able to pick her up?
147 Why is it that my cat does not like having her rump stroked? It seems to hurt her.
149 My cat is purring on my lap one minute and then lashing out at me the next. How can I stop him?

SEE:
27 How do I introduce a new cat to the house where there is one or more already?
27 My new kitten hisses at my dog, although she is used to cats. Will my kitten get used to the dog?
108 My cat keeps getting into fights and developing abscesses. How should they be treated?
127 Why hasn't neutering stopped my male cat from fighting?
136 How do cats communicate with each other?
144 How can I stop my cat from spraying urine around the house?
148 We have two brothers who were inseparable but now fight all the time. What can we do?

SEE:
34 Do Siamese and Burmese cats need any special care?
111 How do I know my queen is 'calling'?
129 Will she stop calling after she has been spayed?
135 Do cats communicate with humans?
135 Can cats understand what their owners are saying?
136 How do cats communicate with each other?
137 Why do cats purr?

SEE:
29 Should I have two kittens rather than a single one?
137 Why does my cat rub his face against my leg?
138 Why does my cat flex its claws and dribble when on my lap?
139 Why does my cat roll on his back when he sees me?

IS THIS BEHAVIOUR RELATED TO YOU, YOUR FAMILY, OR OTHER ANIMALS IN THE HOUSEHOLD?

NO

DOES YOUR CAT GO OUTDOORS?

IS THE BEHAVIOUR NEW OR UNUSUAL FOR YOUR CAT?

YES

NO

IS THE CAT'S BEHAVIOUR DESTRUCTIVE?

YES

NO

YES

NO

YOUR CAT MAY BE SICK.

TRY RETRAINING YOUR CAT IF THIS BEHAVIOUR IS CAUSING PROBLEMS.

YOUR CAT MAY NEED TO GO OUTSIDE, OR BE GIVEN INDOOR EXERCISE, OR BE RETRAINED.

YOUR CAT MAY PREFER BEING AN INDOOR CAT OR MAY BE NERVOUS.

SEE:
51 What should I do if my kitten becomes ill?
67 Why has my cat stopped grooming herself?
82 How will I know when my cat is ill?
82 Why do cats just hide away when they are unwell?
86 Can cats get sunburn?
86 Is it possible for a cat to suffer from heat exhaustion?
87 What are the common causes of poisoning in the cat?
89 My elderly cat has lost her balance. Is this likely to be due to a stroke?

SEE:
134 Why does my cat go crazy over catnip?
140 How can I punish my cat when she misbehaves?
141 I keep having to get my cat down from a tree. He just sits up there and wails. How can I stop him from climbing it?
142 How can I stop my cat from decimating the local wildlife?

SEE:
28 Can feral kittens make good pets?
42 Does my cat need exercise?
42 What exercise can I give my indoor cat?
43 Is it worth buying toys for my indoor cat?
44 Should I get a cat flap?
50 When can my kitten start going outdoors?
108 My cat keeps chewing on electric cables. Is he likely to get electrocuted?
140 How can I stop my cat from climbing the curtains?
140 How can I punish my cat when she misbehaves?
141 My cat is ruining my furniture. What should I do?

SEE:
30 Is it true that Persians make good indoor cats?
44 My new house already has a cat flap, but my stupid cat won't use it!
144 My neutered male cat urinates and defecates in corners. What can I do about it?
144 My nine-month-old male cat goes out but rushes back to use his litter. Should I take it away?
145 My cat is timid and stays indoors all day. How can I get her to go out?
146 My 18-month-old cat won't go outdoors at all. How can I get her used to it?
146 How can I stop my cat from being so nervous?

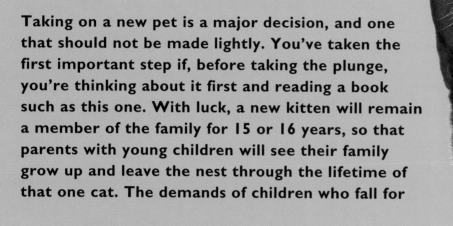

Taking on a new pet is a major decision, and one that should not be made lightly. You've taken the first important step if, before taking the plunge, you're thinking about it first and reading a book such as this one. With luck, a new kitten will remain a member of the family for 15 or 16 years, so that parents with young children will see their family grow up and leave the nest through the lifetime of that one cat. The demands of children who fall for

1 Choosing a Cat

the charms of a fluffy kitten can induce many parents to take on a cat, but the novelty can quickly wear off. Although children should be encouraged to help care for the cat, the cat is the adults' responsibility, and children should not be expected to do all the work.

Some cat owners acquire their new cat by accident, feeding a cat that turns up uninvited, until it eventually makes their home its own. If you are setting out to acquire a cat—rather than simply being chosen by a stray— this chapter aims to provide advice on how to find the perfect pet to fit in with your lifestyle.

your new cat

Practical advice on choosing your new cat, and getting your home ready.

HOW MUCH DOES IT COST TO KEEP A CAT?

- When calculating the cost of keeping a cat you need to consider the following factors:
- Feeding
- Vaccinations
- Neutering
- Parasite control
- Veterinary treatment of any illnesses
- Boarding
- Grooming
- Check the cost of these items, then decide if you can afford to look after a cat before you take on the responsibility.

WHAT DO I NEED TO BUY BEFORE GETTING A KITTEN?

- You will need a cat carrier, to transport your kitten home safely and securely. Get one that is large enough for when your kitten becomes a cat. A plastic carrier is easiest to clean, and, for the kitten's comfort, you can line it with synthetic fur bedding, or just use newspaper and a towel.
- Some attractive cat beds are available, but it is not worth investing a lot of money in a cat bed since your kitten may well have its own views. A closed cardboard box with a hole cut into it and some soft bedding inside is fine, and can be thrown away when it gets dirty.
- You will need a litter tray, at least until your kitten can go outdoors. Many owners prefer a covered tray with a covered lid, and many cats seem to appreciate the extra security that the roof provides. Many kinds of cat litter now have deodorising agents added. Litter tray liners and disposable litter trays are now available to make the task less unpleasant.
- Longhaired kittens will need grooming, and you should start as soon as possible so your kitten becomes accustomed to it. Brushes tend to skim over the knots in the coat, and a fine comb is more effective (see page 68).
- Heavy porcelain feeding bowls are better than plastic ones, as they are less likely to spill and can be more easily cleaned. You'll need one for food and one for water, because although many cats do not drink a great deal, fresh water should be available at all times. If you give your cat tinned food, use a spoon kept separate from your own cutlery.
- A collar is not needed while your kitten is indoors, but buy a collar and tag once it goes outdoors.

IS A PET SHOP THE BEST PLACE TO BUY A KITTEN?

● No, it isn't. I am strongly against the sale of kittens from pet shops:

● Many do not keep the animals in good conditions, and if different litters mix at a vulnerable age, in a poor environment, disease will spread like wildfire. Even if the kittens are well kept, offering them for sale in retail premises encourages impulse purchases by people who feel sorry for kittens, and that is no reason to take on a long-term commitment.

● It is vital that kittens are socialised in a domestic environment before they go to their new homes. A reputable pet shop may keep a register of kittens looking for homes and will put you in touch with someone with a suitable litter.

● I would not advise buying from breeders who keep kittens away from family life.

● If you buy a kitten from a loving home, it stands a good chance of becoming a well-adjusted cat.

ARE KITTENS FROM ANIMAL SHELTERS MORE LIKELY TO CARRY DISEASES?

● Shelters vary greatly in the care and quality of facilities that they are able to provide. Some do an excellent job of taking in and re-homing cats and kittens. Others, often with the very best of intentions, act as hotbeds of infection, in which disease spreads far and wide, causing a great deal of heartache and suffering. Here, even more than in a pet shop, there is the potential for spreading disease among kittens at a very vulnerable stage in their development.

● Despite this, there is a great deal to be said in favour of giving a home to a kitten that might be destroyed, and more so in the case of adult cats, who are more difficult to place in new homes.

● Look for a shelter with a caring staff, where the animals appear well kept and healthy, and where the facilities allow for isolation of the cats so that disease cannot spread from one to another.

IS IT CRUEL TO KEEP CATS IN A FLAT?

● There are varying opinions about this. Some would say it is cruel to allow a cat outdoors and be exposed to the hazards of injury or theft. Most of us believe that a major part of the attraction of owning a cat is the beauty of having an animal that shares its life with us yet is free to come and go as it pleases.

● Many cats fall victim to feline enemy number one—the motor vehicle. Even so, many owners would prefer their cat to have a short and happy life rather than one of confinement. It might be considered cruel suddenly to confine an adult cat that was used to a free life; by contrast, many cats that have lived indoors from kittenhood seem perfectly contented.

● You have to make a decision based on where you live and the type of cat you want.

cats & families

How to establish a compatible and happy relationship with your new cat.

I AM ALLERGIC TO CATS BUT WANT TO OWN ONE. WHICH BREED SHOULD I CONSIDER?

- Unfortunately, cat allergies are not uncommon. Some people find that with a shorthaired non-shedding breed, such as one of the Rex cats, they are fine.
- More commonly, humans are sensitive to a protein found in the saliva that cats spread on their coat when they groom themselves, and frequent bathing of the cat may reduce its effect. It also makes good sense to keep cats out of the bedrooms.
- Medications similar to those used for hay fever in humans may alleviate symptoms, but are not free of side effects.
- There is a desensitisation vaccine under development, but it is not available at the present time.
- In many cases humans have lived with a cat and tolerated the allergic reaction that they have suffered, and then found that it has gradually abated.

- Think carefully about whether you really should be keeping a pet at all. Teddy bears are great for cuddling and so much cheaper to maintain!
- It is not at all unreasonable to leave an adult cat alone during the day, provided it has a cat flap, but a kitten really does need more attention.

MY HUSBAND AND I ARE OUT AT WORK ALL DAY. IS IT ALL RIGHT FOR US TO GET A KITTEN?

- Perhaps you could arrange to have someone come in a couple of times during the day to make sure all is well; or you might think about taking on an adult cat instead of a kitten.
- Believe it or not, it is even possible to purchase videotapes especially designed to keep your cat occupied when you are out, but these are hardly a substitute for human companionship.

A black smoke and white Cornish Rex cat.

IS IT TRUE THAT CATS CAN SMOTHER YOUNG BABIES?

● I used to think that this was just an old wives' tale, but unfortunately there have been confirmed cases of this happening.

● It's not that the cat intends to harm the baby, but cats have a natural desire to find a cosy niche and curl up against something nice and warm. In extremely rare instances, this could obstruct a baby's airway and cause suffocation.

● There is also some evidence to suggest that exposing a young child to high levels of cat hair and dander can predispose him or her to asthma later on in life.

● If you wish to leave the nursery door open, you should cover the cot with a net to keep the cat out.

I HAVE A YOUNG CHILD, AND I'M WORRIED ABOUT TAKING ON A KITTEN. WILL THEY GET ON TOGETHER?

● I'm more concerned about the new kitten than your youngster. Once babies start to become mobile, they seem unable to resist the temptation of giving that fluffy tail a good yank, or pushing a finger down that ear to see how far it can go.

● Most cats are remarkably tolerant of young children and will simply keep out of the way when they feel enough is enough, but a little kitten may not be able to look after itself so well. You will have to keep a close eye on them when they are together.

● The ideal time to get a kitten is when your child is old enough to understand the need to be gentle with a young animal.

● You should also check that your child is not being harmed in any way, due to lack of understanding in handling the kitten.

HOW DO I
INTRODUCE A
NEW CAT TO
THE HOUSE
WHERE THERE
IS ONE OR
MORE
ALREADY?

- Persuading cats to get along with one another is by no means easy, and you should not assume that an existing cat will welcome a newcomer as a friend.
- Cats are naturally territorial creatures, and their first instinct will be to try to chase intruders off their territory.
- A cat used to living with adult cats will be more amenable, especially if the newcomer is a kitten.

- Introducing the cats to each other on neutral territory may be helpful.
- It is possible to buy a cat pheromone spray that mimics the smell of the scent produced by the cheek glands of the cat; even though the scent is not identical to that produced by either cat, spraying helps to relax both the newcomer and the established resident.
- Sometimes the best that can be achieved is a cease-fire, in which each cat works out its own sleeping spots, feeding places, and pathways around the premises. Open hostilities only break out when the cats cannot avoid encountering each other.

MY NEW
KITTEN HISSES
AT MY DOG,
ALTHOUGH
SHE IS USED
TO CATS. WILL
MY KITTEN
GET USED TO
THE DOG?

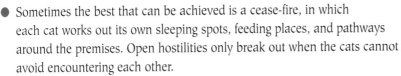

- Unlike getting two cats used to each other, accustoming dogs and cats to each other is generally easier than expected.
- You may find that if you simply let your dog and kitten sort things out, their relationship will settle down—but keep an eye on them from a distance, as your dog could get injured if the kitten takes a swipe at his eyes.

- If this does not seem to be working, you could place the kitten in a wire cat carrier, and then put the kitten in the carrier in the same room as the dog.
- Initially put the carrier well out of the dog's reach, but as they get used to the idea, gradually bring down to floor level. In this way the kitten can get used to the dog and yet feel protected by the cage, and the dog cannot chase the kitten or get scratched. Remain in the same room to make sure that the dog doesn't bark and push the carrier around, frightening the kitten. Eventually leave the lid of the carrier open, so that the kitten can come out when it feels confident enough.

cat nature

Coat colour, breeding, and character can influence your choice of cat.

SHOULD I GET A PEDIGREE OR A CROSSBREED?

- This is very much a matter of personal preference. There is much less difference in temperament and body shape between breeds of cat than between breeds of dog, yet some people are strongly attracted to one particular breed.
- You will have to pay considerably more for a pedigree kitten, and there is some evidence to suggest that a good mishmash of genes makes the average crossbreed somewhat more hardy and perhaps even better balanced psychologically than a pedigree cat.

DO MALE OR FEMALE KITTENS MAKE BETTER PETS?

- Whichever sex you choose, your kitten will need to be neutered (unless you plan to breed it) preferably before it reaches sexual maturity.
- Although there are very big differences between the behaviour patterns of intact males and females, these are much less marked once they have been neutered.
- Male cats tend to be more independently-minded, and so spend more time out and about than females. Some people feel that female cats are more affectionate, but there are plenty of stay-at-home, affectionate male cats.
- All in all, the sex of your kitten is not of any great importance when you make your choice—unless you want kittens, in which case a queen is the only choice.

Pedigree Tonkinese kittens

Crossbred kittens

- Feral cats are not actually wild cats, but are simply domestic cats that have adapted to living away from a household environment. Just about any cat has the capacity to become feral should the necessity arise.
- Rather than trying to eradicate colonies of feral cats, most cat welfare organisations have a policy of trapping, neutering and releasing adults in their original colony, and re-homing kittens.
- If a kitten from a feral environment is to become a truly domesticated pet, it is essential that it be taken into its new environment as soon as possible—ideally, as soon as it is weaned, at around six weeks of age.
- It is possible to take on older feral kittens or even adult cats, but they will always retain a wild streak, and are unlikely to feel at ease if confined indoors or picked up and restrained.

CAN FERAL KITTENS MAKE GOOD PETS?

- I used to say there was only one thing better than a new kitten, and that's two new kittens, until I took on two brothers who grew to hate each other as they grew up!
- More commonly, cats that grow up together become inseparable, and it is certainly most enjoyable to see them playing and socialising with each other.
- Studies have shown that cats in a multi-cat household do tend to be a bit less human-oriented, so if you want a cat that considers you as the centre of its universe, keep just one.
- On the other hand, if you are out a lot, there is much to be said for getting a pair of kittens.

SHOULD I HAVE TWO KITTENS RATHER THAN A SINGLE ONE?

WHAT IS THE NATURAL COAT COLOUR OF THE DOMESTIC CAT?

- All the varied colours of our domestic cats have evolved from just one colour—the striped tabby. This colouring offers the best camouflage among vegetation.
- Even black cats are actually tabbies genetically, but the agouti (lighter) bands are changed to black. This can be seen in black kittens, where 'ghost' stripes can often be seen over the body.
- In Europe, the blotched, or classic, tabby has overtaken the striped tabby, or mackerel, as the most common cat colouring, but this variation is relatively recent, and has become prevalent in Britain only since Elizabethan times.

ARE TORTOISESHELL CATS ALWAYS FEMALE AND GINGER CATS ALWAYS MALE?

IS IT TRUE THAT WHITE CATS ARE OFTEN DEAF?

- Almost. Tortoiseshell cats result from a genetic mixture of orange (sometimes called yellow) and black.
- The genes causing the tortoiseshell colouring are found on the X chromosome, and two X chromosomes with matching tortoiseshell genes must be present to produce a tortoiseshell kitten.
- Only the female has two X chromosomes (the male has an X and a smaller Y chromosome).
- It is therefore only a male with a genetic abnormality – two X chromosomes in addition to the Y one – that has tortoiseshell colouring. These mixed-up tortoiseshell cats may have male sex organs, but they are infertile and so unable to breed. In the case of ginger cats, these can be either male or female.

- Yes. A hereditary form of deafness which may affect one or both ears is often seen in white cats with blue eyes, and sometimes white orange-eyed cats. The disability is likely to be passed to future generations.
- These cats often do not make good mothers, as they cannot hear their kittens, and they should certainly not be let out near a road.

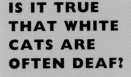

pedigree cats

Profiles the characteristics of many different breeds to help you make an informed choice.

WHAT BREED OF CAT SHOULD I CHOOSE?

- This is an almost impossible question to answer, because if you have decided to get a pedigree cat, it's a matter of personal choice as to which breed you prefer.
- If you are unsure, purchase a book that specialises in pedigree cats or, better still, visit a cat show, where you will see many breeds in the flesh (or fur) and can talk to breeders about their particular breed of cat.

HOW CAN I FIND A GOOD BREEDER?

- You should be able to find out more about local breeders from your vet.
- Each breed has a Breed Society, whose address is available from the governing bodies. In the United Kingdom, the Governing Council of the Cat Fancy (GCCF) is the largest cat register. In the United States, try the Cat Fanciers' Association or the American Cat Association. The Canadian Cat Association is the only register in Canada.
- Many cat fancier magazines carry advertisements from breeders; or, if you are connected to the Internet, you could look online.
- Personal recommendation is the most valuable source of information for finding someone who really cares about his or her kittens.

IS IT TRUE THAT PERSIANS MAKE GOOD INDOOR CATS?

- The Persian has a placid nature which seems to adapt well to life indoors and makes them one of the most popular pedigree breeds of cat. With its long, silky coat, flattened face, and large, orange eyes, it is a very attractive cat, with a wide range of coat colours.
- A life indoors will certainly make it easier to manage the coat, which requires daily attention to keep it free of knots.
- Some experts are concerned that selective breeding has interfered with the hardy nature of the cat and advise prospective purchasers to avoid the Ultra type of Persian, which has been bred with an extremely flat face. This bone structure can interfere with breathing and vision.

IS IT TRUE THAT THE TURKISH VAN CAT LIKES WATER?

- This breed originates from the vicinity of Lake Van in southeast Turkey.
- Vans are unique among domestic cats in that they have a natural affinity for water and can even be proficient swimmers.
- They also have a coat that becomes thicker and longer during the cold winter months, but they are easier to groom than Persian cats because they do not have the same thick, woolly undercoat.

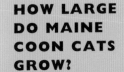

HOW LARGE DO MAINE COON CATS GROW?

- This was the first longhaired breed to be produced naturally in North America, and it is one of the largest breeds of cat. A male can weigh up to 8 kg (18 pounds), about twice the average weight of a domestic cat.
- They are hardy cats, with a dense, rugged coat that protects them from the extremes of weather found in their native East Coast environment. They have large ears, a strong and muscular body and powerful legs.
- The Maine Coon is an ideal pet for someone looking for a strong and confident cat.

DO BENGAL CATS MAINTAIN THE CHARACTERISTICS OF THEIR WILD RELATIVES?

- This cat was derived from an American breeding programme in 1963, in which a breeder crossed a male domestic cat with a female Asian leopard cat she had bought from a pet store. The aim was to produce a domestic breed with striking leopard markings. Offspring with sound temperament were selected, and the breed is now popular, although costly.
- Any kittens bought as pets will be generations away from the original leopard cat crosses, (which tended to be timid or aggressive), and are usually sociable, making excellent pets. Bengals are becoming increasingly popular at cat shows, and the GCCF has set up official show standards for each type.

DO MANX CATS SUFFER BECAUSE OF THEIR LACK OF TAIL?

Spotted tabby and white, rumpy Manx cat.

IS THE ABYSSINIAN CAT THE ANCESTOR OF ALL OUR CURRENT DOMESTIC CATS?

- It is unclear whether the Abyssinian cat is descended from the ancient Egyptian cats, but it certainly bears a striking resemblance in body type and colour to the cats so widely worshipped, painted and sculpted by the Egyptians many thousands of years ago.
- Its history as a pedigree domestic cat can be traced back to cats brought back to Britain from Africa at the end of the Abyssinian war in the 1860s.
- The domestic cat itself is thought to have evolved from the African Wild Cat, which can be found in savanna and bush regions of that continent.

- Manx cats originate from the Isle of Man, off England's west coast, where a reserve has been set up to maintain them in their native environment.
- They can be found with varying degrees of taillessness. Stumpies have a very short tail; rumpies, absolutely no tail at all; and rumpy-risers, just the slightest bump of a tail. Longies have tails almost as long as the average cat.
- This is a hereditary deformity that is not without problems. Apart from the fact that the tail is a very useful organ that helps with coordination of movement and communication with other cats, its absence often leads to spinal deformations.
- Many Manx cats have an abnormal hopping gait on their hind legs, and some have more serious deformations such as spina bifida, in which the roof of the spinal canal fails to fuse together properly. Severely affected fetuses may be aborted before birth.
- The Manx standard disqualifies any cat with congenital deformities. Careful breeding can help eliminate or minimise these defects.

Stumpy Manx cat with tabby markings.

HOW DID REX CATS GET THEIR CURLY COAT?

- The two most common breeds of Rex cat originated in the United Kingdom with mutations in hair growth that turned up in individual cats. These characteristics were carefully nurtured by breeding programmes to produce distinct pedigree lines.
- The first of these was the Cornish Rex, bred from a cat called Kallibunker in the 1950s. The Devon Rex has a more tightly twisted coat and was bred from a smoky-gray cat called Kirlee in the 1960s.
- Other mutations have appeared in other countries, but none have been developed into specific breeds to the same extent.
- Some people who are allergic to other cats' hair find that they are able to keep Rex cats.

I'VE HEARD THAT THERE ARE NOW HAIRLESS CATS. ISN'T IT CRUEL TO BREED THEM WITHOUT HAIR?

- There is no doubt that the Sphynx cat is otherworldly in appearance, with a body that is totally bald except for small amounts of short, downy hair at the extremities.
- Developed in Ontario from a single black and white hairless kitten born in 1966, it is now becoming more widely available in Europe and North America, although many cat associations refuse to recognise it as a breed.
- Its lack of coat would severely hamper its ability to survive out of doors in the way that most domestic cats still could, suffering both from exposure to cold and to sunburn from ultraviolet radiation.
- Although requiring a cat to be hairless is not cruel, some experts consider it a shame to breed cats so far removed from their ancestors, in order to cater to a taste for the exotic.

- Siamese and Burmese are the two most popular examples of what are known as oriental cats, with leaner and lither bodies than their Western counterparts.
- Their physical needs are no different from that of any other pedigree cat, but their behavioural characteristics make particular demands upon their owners.
- Siamese and, to a slightly lesser extent, Burmese, are very vocal, extroverted cats who will complain loudly if they do not get the love and attention they consider they need.
- They are suited to owners who want a human-oriented cat and have the time and patience to indulge their needs.

DO SIAMESE AND BURMESE CATS NEED ANY SPECIAL CARE?

Seal-point Siamese.

Blue Burmese.

- They are Siamese cats without the Siamese colourings, such as the dark points and blue eyes.
- This may seem a contradiction in terms, but when the first Siamese cats were imported into the West, some had a solid body colour, but this was thought undesirable, and they quickly died out.
- In the 1950s, an effort was made to recreate this type of cat, producing varieties such as the Foreign Black, the Foreign Blue, and the Havana. The latter is a cat with a coat colour very similar to the brown Burmese cat, but with the considerably lither and more elongated body of the Siamese breed.

WHAT ARE ORIENTAL SHORTHAIR CATS?

IS THERE ANY DIFFERENCE BETWEEN MIXED-BREED CATS AND PEDIGREE SHORTHAIR CATS?

- There certainly is if you are a breeder of pedigree shorthair cats, but to most people they may look amazingly similar, apart from the price.
- Both British and American Shorthair cats have been developed into breeds, with British Shorthairs having slightly rounder faces and smaller bodies than their American counterparts. They have a denser coat than many non-pedigree cats, and are bred in an unusual range of pure colours.

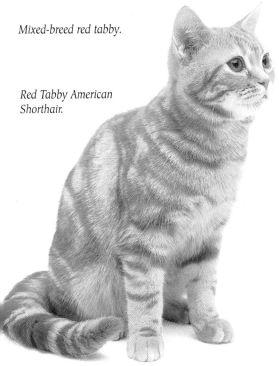

Mixed-breed red tabby.

Red Tabby American Shorthair.

Cream British Shorthair.

Cats are fairly easy pets to keep, but knowing what makes your cat tick will help you to care for its needs. It is enjoyable for us, as cat owners, to understand how this originally wild animal has adapted so well to living side-by-side with humans.

Although both cats and dogs are carnivores that have become domesticated, the cat is far more specialised, with a body that is perfectly adapted to stalking and killing its prey during the twilight hours. Whereas a dog relies mainly on its sense of smell in hunting, cats are more dependent on sight. Their sense of balance and their coordination are extremely refined, and their long canine teeth and sharp

2 General Care & Training

claws are lethal weapons for killing prey. The sleek body of the cat is designed for stealth and speed, not for stamina and a long chase. The metabolism of the cat has lost many of the mechanisms that enable the liver to utilise vegetable-based sources of certain essential nutrients, making the cat an obligate carnivore. This also means that the cat's liver cannot break down poisons and drugs, so that some drugs, such as aspirin, and household compounds, which are safe for other species, are toxic to the cat. This chapter answers questions about adapting your cat's behaviour in the home.

safety first

How to protect your cat from traffic and other potential dangers.

I LIVE ON A BUSY ROAD. HOW CAN I KEEP MY CAT SAFE?

- This is a difficult problem, and most owners just allow their cats to take their chances. Most cats will develop road sense in a fairly short time.
- Other owners go to the opposite extreme and attempt to keep their cats indoors all the time.
- An ideal compromise, if you have the resources, is to enclose part or all of your garden, and give your cat access to this area via a cat flap, but not to the road. Such an enclosure will also prevent your cat from fighting with other cats.
- Fencing to confine a cat in the garden should be high, and it should have either a mesh roof or an overhang to keep cats from climbing over.

IS IT SAFE TO ALLOW MY CAT OUT ONTO THE BALCONY OF MY FLAT?

- It is not uncommon for cats to fall off flat balconies, and despite their reputation for being able to land on their feet, serious or even fatal injuries can and do result from such falls.
- If you live in a flat and want your cat to be able to go out onto your balcony as an alternative to going outdoors, you should consider putting up mesh to make the balcony cat-friendly.

Cats enjoy being able to explore outside, especially where there is extra entertainment.

- A cat collar with a name tag is essential for quick identification, but it runs the risk of getting lost or even removed.
- There are two main methods of permanently identifying your cat.
- An ear can be tattooed with a number that is held on a central register. This requires a general anaesthetic, and it may become difficult to read with time, but it has the advantage of being fairly obvious when the cat is examined.

WHAT IS THE BEST WAY OF IDENTIFYING MY CAT IN CASE OF LOSS OR INJURY?

- Implantable microchips are now available; these are about the size of a grain of rice and are injected under the skin of the scruff of the neck with a needle. Each microchip is encoded with a unique number which can then be keyed into a central database to track down the owner's identity. For more information, ask your vet.

- It is possible for a cat to snag its collar on something such as a branch, and either asphyxiate itself or be unable to escape.

CAN CAT COLLARS BE DANGEROUS?

- However, a collar can provide a crucial form of identification should your cat become lost or injured, and the value of this will override any hazard.
- Make sure that any collar you purchase has either an elastic section that will stretch and allow the cat to slip out if necessary, or a snap release, so that the catch will snap open if excessive force is applied.

Inserting a microchip.

Ear tattooing.

- It's not surprising that most cats detest the sight of their cat carrier. For years they have become conditioned to realise that when this object comes out of the closet it means one of two things—a trip to the cattery or a trip to the vet. Neither is an attractive option to the average cat.

- You can prevent this negative reaction by getting your cat accustomed to going into the carrier at other times, perhaps putting some tasty treats into it to add extra attraction and interest.

- Some carriers split into an upper and a lower half and can double as a bed for your cat.

- Spraying a feline pheromone extract into the carrier will also help to make it more appealing.

- Even with this obstacle overcome, your problems may not be over: when you arrive at the vet's you then face the task of getting the cat to come out of the carrier!

HOW DO I GET MY CAT INTO A CAT CARRIER?

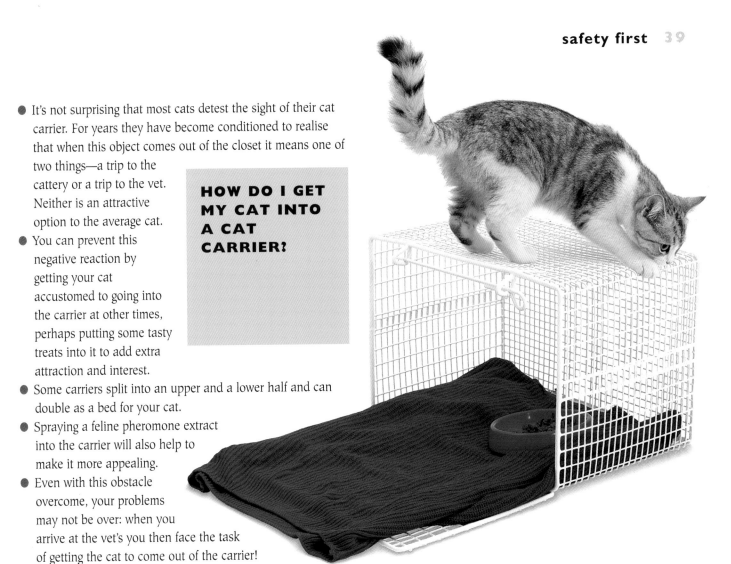

IS IT BEST TO SEDATE CATS FOR TRANSPORTING?

- In my experience, sedatives are unreliable for use on cats, and the effect that they have on an individual cat cannot be predicted with any confidence. Perversely, some cats even seem to become hyperactive, rather than sedated, when they are given certain drugs.

- Generally speaking, a sturdy cat carrier is all that is required.

- If your cat is very excitable and you are determined to try to administer a sedative, you should get a supply from your vet well before you travel, so that you can try out the recommended dose in advance of your journey to see what effect it has.

- If your cat is prone to travel sickness, it is best not to feed it for a few hours beforehand. There are drugs to suppress vomiting that work quite well on cats.

HOW DO I MAKE SURE MY CAT DOES NOT RUN OFF WHEN I MOVE TO A NEW HOME?

- There are all sorts of old wives' tales about this one; one ploy is to butter your cat's paws. I'd save your butter, and simply keep your cat confined indoors until it seems settled.

- Some cats settle down within a matter of a few days; others can take a few weeks. Wait until they are strolling around your new home happily and confidently.

- When you do take the plunge, make sure your cat is wearing a collar and tag bearing your new address or telephone number, and let your cat out just before feeding time, so that it will quickly be back looking for food.

house

training

How to house train your kitten or cat

SHOULD I DISINFECT THE CAT'S LITTER TRAY?

- It is important to keep the litter tray clean to prevent the buildup of bacteria that cause infection, but you may find that strong-smelling disinfectants may deter your cat from using it.
- Use a disinfectant that is known to be safe for cats. Many products can be purchased from pet shops, or you can use a weak solution of bleach with washing-up liquid in hot water. Rinse the tray out thoroughly afterwards.

HOW DO I GET MY CAT TO USE THE LITTER TRAY?

- This is something that most cats seem to take to surprisingly easily if they are simply restricted to an area indoors where a tray has been left.
- If you are experiencing problems, you could try experimenting with different types of commercial litter. In Britain, most are based upon fuller's earth, a type of clay. Your cat may have a preference for a certain type. You could even try adding some earth from the garden, to give the tray that authentic aroma your cat appreciates.
- Make sure that the tray is positioned in a site with easy access for your cat, yet in a spot that is reasonably secluded, as many cats feel vulnerable when they perform in a tray, and may not use it if it has been placed in a very exposed position. Some appreciate the privacy of a tray that is equipped with a commodious cover.

WHEN MY CAT URINATES HE SPRAYS HIGH, SO IT GOES OVER THE EDGE OF THE LITTER TRAY. WHAT IS THE ANSWER?

- If the tray is in a corner, you could try putting aluminium foil against the walls, but there is a danger that the sound of his urine hitting the foil may frighten him so much that he may refuse to use the tray altogether.
- It may be simplest to purchase a litter tray that comes with a top, so that the cat enters via a hole, and any urine sprayed against the sides will run down into the tray.
- Of course, the whole contraption will then need cleaning regularly.

MY PREGNANT WIFE SAYS SHE SHOULD NOT EMPTY LITTER TRAYS. IS IT TRUE, OR IS SHE TRYING TO DRAG ME AWAY FROM THE FOOTBALL GAME?

- I'm afraid that your wife does have some justification for what she is saying.
- Cats, especially kittens, can carry an organism called *toxoplasma*. This is a tiny single-celled parasite that causes no more than mild diarrhoea in cats but can pose a serious health hazard to an unborn child.
- Human exposure to this agent is very common, and the disease is quite rare because most people rapidly develop an immunity.
- It is thought that the most common source of human infection is handling or eating undercooked meat, so although there is no need to panic about the hazard, I am sure you would rather take a break from the football than put your new baby at any unnecessary risk.

HOW CAN I TRAIN MY CAT TO RELIEVE ITSELF OUTDOORS?

- Some cats become so used to using their litter trays that they refuse to perform anywhere else, and will come rushing indoors if they feel the urge. This is particularly common in young cats that have just started going outdoors, and will often correct itself naturally.
- In some cases, however, this behaviour persists, and many owners resent having to clean out the tray.
- Do not remove the litter tray, as the cat may then start urinating elsewhere indoors, and this can be a difficult habit to break once it starts.
- Leave a door open when the cat is out, and move the litter tray toward the outdoors step by step. You can even spread some used cat litter in the parts of the yard that you don't mind your cat using as a toilet area.
- Once your cat gets used to using the litter tray outside, you can then safely remove the tray entirely.

exercise

How to keep your cat active, energetic, and healthy.

DOES MY CAT NEED EXERCISE?

- Exercise is important, especially for young cats, because unless their energy can be channelled in a positive way, they can become destructive and start damaging the furnishings.
- Apart from helping to prevent obesity, exercise helps to tone the muscles and keep the cardiovascular system in good working order (although it should be noted that cats do not suffer from clogging of the arteries with fatty deposits as humans do).
- Some evidence suggests that certain diseases, such as diabetes mellitus (sugar diabetes) and urinary problems, are more common in overweight and lazy cats.

WHAT EXERCISE CAN I GIVE MY INDOOR CAT?

- Various companies manufacture indoor exercise structures for cats—stimulating, multilevel areas where they can climb, perch at a height, scratch and play with various hanging objects. Some of these are very elaborate and, needless to say, very expensive. If you're at all handy with tools, it's not too difficult to make something yourself.
- Whatever you provide, it is essential that indoor cats do have somewhere suitable to scratch, because they need to pull off the outer worn part of their claws to expose the new, sharp ones underneath. If you do not provide something for this purpose, you can be sure your cat will start to use your furniture instead.
- The most important thing that you can give your indoor cat, however, is your time, for they are much more dependent upon human companionship than cats who are free to go in and out as they please.

IS IT WORTH BUYING TOYS FOR MY INDOOR CAT?

- Owners love to buy toys for their pets, and many cats receive a Christmas stocking full of treats because their owners do not want them to feel left out. More often than not, this is for the benefit of the owner rather than the cat.
- Toys that are likely to appeal to cats are those that bring out their hunting instincts, such as a 'spider on a stick' which cats love to swipe at with their paws. Some cats' toys are impregnated with catnip, which many cats find intoxicating.
- Very elaborate toys are likely to be a waste of money; like toddlers, cats often get more pleasure playing with the packaging than with the contents.
- The simplest of toys, such as a table tennis ball, or a little fluffy toy on a piece of string, are often the most successful.

- Yes. There is always a danger that a cat will swallow something that can cause problems.
- Obviously, any toys should be nontoxic, but it is also important that they do not have buttons or any other small parts that can be pulled off by the cat and then swallowed.
- Sometimes kittens will start to chew and then may swallow lengths of string or wool, This should be discouraged, as it can cause a serious intestinal blockage.
- Even more dangerous is thread with a needle on the end, which a kitten could swallow while playing.
  Just as with young children, you have to be
- constantly vigilant to make sure that anything potentially harmful is kept out of their way.

CAN SOME TOYS BE HARMFUL?

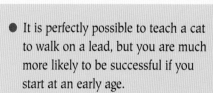

CAN I TEACH MY CAT TO WALK ON A LEAD?

- It is perfectly possible to teach a cat to walk on a lead, but you are much more likely to be successful if you start at an early age.
- Many cats feel exposed walking along the street, but a harness and lead is very useful as a means of preventing escape if you want to travel with your cat.

- A cat flap would obviously make access into and out of your home much easier for your cat, and save your having to jump up and down on command when your pet wants to go out for a stroll.
- However, it does mean that you lose a great deal of control over when your cat does go in and out, although most flaps are lockable, so that you can shut them to keep your cat in at night, for example.
- Some nervous cats dislike a flap because they feel that their home territory is threatened by possible invasion by other cats, and this can cause problems such as urine marking indoors.

SHOULD I GET A CAT FLAP?

MY NEW HOUSE ALREADY HAS A CAT FLAP, BUT MY STUPID CAT WON'T USE IT!

- Cats that do not become accustomed to cat flaps at an early age—usually by following their mother through one—often do find the concept difficult to grasp; so you can rest assured that your cat is not uniquely stupid.
- The answer is to jam the flap in the open position, so that your cat can go through it without having to push the flap. If necessary, you can wait until your cat is hungry, and place a bowl of food just outside.
- Once your cat has got used to going through the flap it's a minor step for it to master pushing the flap open.
- Some flaps are made of transparent plastic, which many cats find more approachable.

HOW CAN I STOP OTHER CATS FROM COMING IN THROUGH OUR CAT FLAP?

- This can be a major problem if a cat feels that its territory is being invaded and you may not wish to provide hospitality for other cats.
- Manufacturers have tried to overcome this by making flaps that are activated by a strong magnet attached to the cat's collar. This usually works well, although a cat that is equipped with one of these collars for its own flap will be able to gain entry through other magnetised flaps, too.
- Also, I have occasionally heard of problems where the cat's collar has caught on metallic fittings in the flap.
- As always, the collar should have an elastic section to allow for quick release if it becomes snagged.

holidays

Making provision for cat care while you are away on holiday.

CAN I LEAVE MY CAT ALONE AT HOME WHEN I GO ON HOLIDAY?

- Only if you have a reliable friend or neighbour who is prepared to come in at least twice a day to check that all is well, provide fresh food and water, and take responsibility for obtaining any veterinary treatment that may become necessary.

CAN I TAKE MY CAT AWAY ON HOLIDAY WITH ME?

- It's certainly possible, although if you are crossing into another country you should find out if there are any regulations regarding the transit of animals across their borders.
- You also need to make certain that your cat will be welcome at your final destination.
- Cats that are accustomed to travelling, and particularly those used to wearing a harness, are likely to adjust well.
- The main danger is that the cat will escape in strange territory and get lost.
- You should make sure the cat is wearing a collar and tag with an address where you can be contacted.

MY CAT IS DIABETIC AND NEEDS REGULAR INJECTIONS. WHAT CAN I DO WHEN I GO AWAY?

- It is absolutely essential that diabetic cats receive their injections regularly.
- Catteries are often reluctant to take on this degree of responsibility, so if another member of your family is not able to take on the task, you should inquire as to whether your veterinary clinic is able to board your cat while you are away. Most vets are able to offer this type of service to their clients.

A diabetic cat having a health check before being boarded at a veterinary clinic.

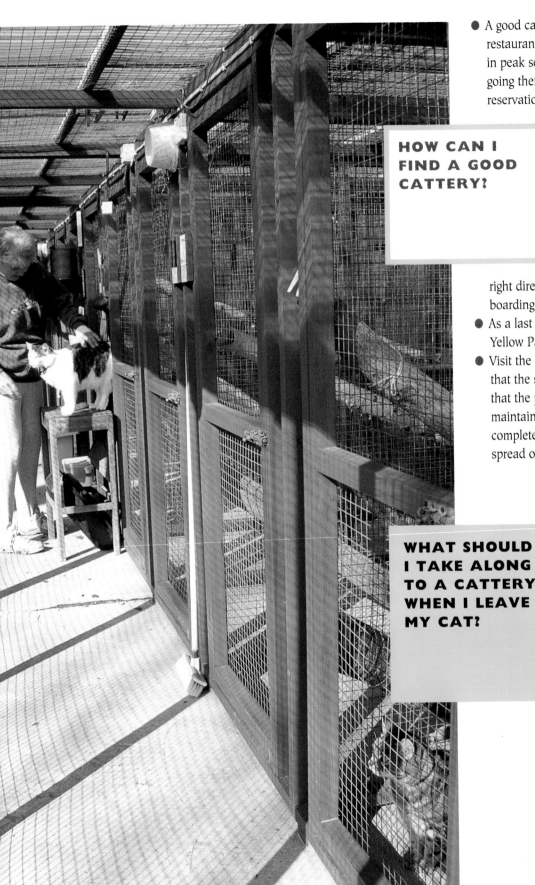

A good cattery is a bit like a good restaurant—if you can get in at short notice in peak season, then it's probably not worth going there in the first place! Make your reservations well in advance, particularly if you are going away during school holidays, when demand is heaviest.

HOW CAN I FIND A GOOD CATTERY?

- Recommendation from friends who have used a particular cattery is always the best way of finding a good one; or your vet may be able to point you in the right direction, or might even offer cat boarding on his or her premises.
- As a last resort, you can look in your local Yellow Pages directory.
- Visit the cattery beforehand to make sure that the staff seem caring and well trained, that the premises are clean and well maintained, and that the facilities allow complete separation of cats to prevent the spread of disease.

WHAT SHOULD I TAKE ALONG TO A CATTERY WHEN I LEAVE MY CAT?

- Don't take too many items, or some things will be lost.
- The cattery may encourage you to take a cat bed, if you have one, and perhaps one or two favourite toys.

WILL THE CATTERY INSIST ON VACCINATIONS?

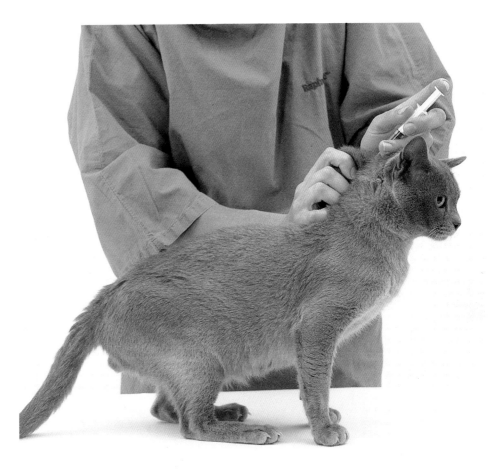

- Any reputable cattery will ask to see your cat's vaccination certificate, which should be shown to be updated and signed by your vet.
- Most catteries insist upon vaccinations for rabies, feline distemper (panleukopaenia), feline upper respiratory disease, feline leukaemia virus, and feline infectious peritonitis.
- This may require a course of two vaccinations three weeks apart if your annual boosters have run out of date. Check with the cattery in advance.

- You will probably be asked to sign a form giving the cattery management permission to obtain any veterinary treatment that may be deemed necessary in your absence, although they will also normally ask for a telephone number where they can contact you if any problems arise.
- They should also request your own vet's name and telephone number, so that your cat's relevant medical history can be checked out.
- The cost of any treatment will be at your expense, unless you take out insurance to cover such an eventuality.

WHAT IF MY CAT SHOULD BECOME ILL WHILE I AM ON HOLIDAY?

WHAT IF I AM DISSATISFIED WITH THE CARE MY CAT RECEIVED AT A CATTERY?

- Initially you should take this up with the management of the cattery; but if you do not receive any satisfaction from them, you should report it to the licensing authority in your area.
- If you still do not receive a satisfactory response, you can consult a lawyer.

From birth to three weeks of age, a kitten is dependent on its mother, but then it will explore and play with its brothers and sisters. By 5 weeks of age, senses of sight, hearing, taste, smell, and touch are developed, and by 8 weeks the kitten should be weaned. Kittens have their final vaccinations at 16 weeks, and soon after that they can start to explore outdoors. Unless the cat's sexual development is interrupted by neutering, cats reach maturity at six months. Males assert their superiority over other cats, and females will produce and rear their own litter.

There is no direct association between human years and feline ones—and it's certainly not true to say that one cat year equals seven human years.

A cat is elderly when it reaches its teens. Digestion and absorption of food is

3 Kitten to Elderly Cat

impaired, kidney function is reduced, and senses become less acute. The skin becomes dry and flaky, and the coat less shiny. The metabolic rate slows, hormone production is reduced, and the cat is less able to regulate its body temperature. Some cats put on weight, but elderly cats may lose weight because they are not able to extract enough nutrition from their food. Mobility is reduced, and the cat will spend more time indoors in front of a fire. Aged cats dislike changes in their routine, and will protest loudly if all is not to their liking.

vaccinations

The range of vaccines and their effectiveness in preventing disease.

- We are now able to prevent several very serious infectious diseases in cats by means of vaccination, and every kitten should receive a veterinary examination and vaccination course before being allowed

WHICH VACCINATIONS DOES MY NEW KITTEN NEED?

access to the great outdoors. The diseases that are covered by the vaccination course should be:

- *Feline infectious enteritis,* or *feline panleukopaenia.* This disease is caused by a virus that produces very severe vomiting and diarrhoea, with a very high mortality rate. It is becoming much less common nowadays due to the effectiveness of this vaccine.

- *Cat flu* (see page 95) can be caused by several infectious agents, but the two most common, feline calicivirus and feline upper respiratory disease complex, are always included in a vaccine. This provides fairly good protection against infection, and although it is possible for a vaccinated cat to contract an infection, this is usually much milder than if the cat hadn't been vaccinated.

- *Feline leukaemia virus* (see page 95) can cause a wide range of illnesses in cats, including cancer. The vaccine has become available only in the last decade, but it is recommended for kittens, as they are very susceptible to the virus at this age.

- *Rabies.* This is mandatory in most areas where rabies is endemic, because the virus not only is very serious in cats but can be lethal if transmitted to humans. Fortunately, the vaccine is very safe and effective.

- There are vaccines against other agents, such as chlamydia, which can cause chronic conjunctivitis and flu-like signs in cats, and coronavirus, which is the cause of *feline infectious peritonitis* (see page 96). The present vaccine against coronavirus is not very reliable, so is not in widespread use at this time, but it is hoped that a more effective vaccine will become available in the future.

ARE VACCINES COMPLETELY SAFE AND 100 PERCENT EFFECTIVE?

- No vaccine, human or animal, can ever claim to be 100 percent safe or 100 percent effective, but we are fortunate that modern veterinary vaccines today are now very pure, and much less likely to cause any kind of reaction than was previously the case.

- From time to time a cat will seem a bit unwell after vaccination, and in some cases this may persist for a few days.

- It is possible for cats to develop an allergic reaction, which usually takes the form of a swollen face and limbs very soon after the injection; this should be treated by a vet without delay.

- Some vaccines are known to be more effective than others, but even those that are very reliable may not take properly if the cat has an immune system disorder.

- It is possible for a cat to carry feline leukaemia virus without showing any signs of ill health. If such a cat is vaccinated against the virus, the vaccine is not likely to do any harm, but it will not prevent the cat from becoming infected.

- Some vets advise blood-testing cats before vaccination; others warn owners about the chance of their cat being a carrier. The latter is a reasonable option in view of the trouble and expense involved in carrying out the test, provided that owners realise that cats may test positive for the virus despite vaccination.

SHOULD MY CAT BE BLOOD-TESTED FOR LEUKAEMIA VIRUS BEFORE BEING VACCINATED?

MY KITTEN WILL BE LIVING INDOORS. DOES SHE NEED TO BE VACCINATED?

- A cat that is completely isolated from all other cats does not have any chance of contracting any of the diseases against which we can vaccinate, apart from the very slim possibility that humans carry an infection indirectly.

- However, if a cat that leads a very sheltered existence should suddenly be exposed to a virus, that cat will have very little resistance to infection—compared to a cat that goes out and about and boosts its immunity by repeated exposure to small amounts of the virus—and would probably contract a very severe infection.

- There is always a risk that a housebound cat may escape outdoors or come into contact with infection when being taken to a veterinary clinic, so it is advisable that all cats receive regular vaccinations and booster injections.

- This varies with the vaccination programme that your vet uses, but usually kittens are given the first injection at or after nine weeks, and the second one three weeks later. At least a week must elapse before the vaccine has had a chance to have its full effect.

WHEN CAN MY KITTEN START GOING OUTDOORS?

- Provided that a female cat is spayed at around five months of age, she is not likely to come into season and get pregnant if she goes outdoors.

- However, some owners do decide to keep their kittens in until they are older than 13 weeks.

- Some of the diseases that we vaccinate against, such as feline panleukopaenia, are more common in younger cats, but there is no age at which a particular cat is no longer susceptible.

DOES MY CAT NEED BOOSTER VACCINATIONS THROUGHOUT HER LIFE?

- As your cat gets older, the annual health check that your vet provides as part of the vaccination procedure becomes more important. An elderly cat that contracts a preventable infection may be affected more seriously than a younger animal.

- It is best that cats receive annual booster injections throughout their lives.

A curious blue tabby kitten in a potting shed shows the dangers that a young cat may encounter when exploring new territory.

kitten to cat

How to care for and handle young kittens, and fascinating facts about cats.

WHAT SHOULD I DO IF MY KITTEN BECOMES ILL?

- Kittens do not have large reserves of energy and can go downhill very rapidly if they are ill, although it is also true to say that they can bounce back very quickly once they are on the road to recovery.
- It's normal for a kitten to spend quite a bit of its time snoozing—apparently practising for when it grows up—but the catnaps should be interspersed with periods of frenzied activity as the kitten looks around for some fun.
- If this normal pattern of behaviour changes, and particularly if the kitten goes off its food, or shows some more specific signs of illness, such as sneezing, coughing, vomiting, or diarrhoea, you should obtain prompt veterinary advice.

WHAT IS THE CORRECT WAY TO PICK UP A KITTEN?

- You can pick up a small kitten by scooping it up with a hand under its abdomen, but as it gets larger, it is important to help support its weight with your other hand under its hindquarters.
- If a kitten is really struggling and you need to restrain it, you will do no harm if you do as its mother would do and grasp a handful of skin over the scruff of its neck.

Picking up your kitten so that it feels secure and comfortable.

HOW ACCURATELY CAN YOU TELL THE AGE OF A CAT?

● It is very difficult to age a cat accurately, except at about five months, when the temporary canine teeth are shed and replaced with permanent ones.
● With older cats, it is only possible to make an informed guess on the basis of the cat's body condition—in particular, the amount of tartar that has accumulated on its teeth.
● Cats age at different rates, and even to the experienced eye, one five-year-old cat can look much the same as a cat twice its age.

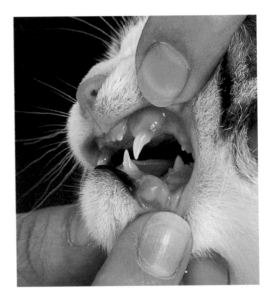

Temporary canine of 12-week-old kitten.

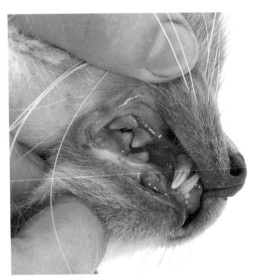

Accumulation of tartar on elderly cat's teeth.

HOW LONG CAN I EXPECT MY CAT TO LIVE?

● A female tabby cat called 'Ma' was put to sleep in November 1957 at the age of 34 in Drewsteignton, Devon, in England, but it is claimed that another Devon-resident tabby, called 'Puss', died the day after his 36th birthday in November 1939.
● Despite these record-breaking statistics, it is unusual for a cat to live into its twenties. Many cats die at an early age due to road accidents, which brings the average life expectancy straight down; but among those that learn how to cope with the traffic or are kept off the street, living to the age of 15 or 16 is not uncommon.

I HAVE ADOPTED A FEMALE CAT. HOW CAN I TELL IF SHE HAS BEEN SPAYED?

● If she has been spayed recently, it should be simple to see the scar, or the place where the hair has been clipped away at the operation site on the cat's left flank. In the US, the scar would be in the middle of the abdomen (just below the navel).
● If she was spayed some time ago, it may be possible to feel the scar, but often there is no way of knowing.
● The only safe course of action in these circumstances is to keep the cat indoors for six months, away from any possible mates, to see if she comes into season.

aging cat

Ensuring that your elderly cat continues to live a happy life.

- It is not uncommon for cats to wander off to a new home if all is not to their liking, but I can understand why you are upset if you have cared for them for 13 years and they have decided the cuisine is better elsewhere.
- You could try putting down a bowl of dry catfood so that they can help themselves during the course of the day.
- The only other alternative is to have a gentle word with your neighbour and discuss the problem you are having. Your neighbour may be totally unaware that you are upset and may be willing to stop putting out food.

WHAT EXTRA CARE DOES AN ELDERLY CAT NEED?

- As described earlier in this chapter, there are many bodily changes that occur in old age that affect both physical and mental function. Many veterinary practices run senior pet programmes which offer an in-depth checkup for older cats. This will usually include a blood test to show up problems such as kidney disease as early as possible. Apart from keeping a vigilant watch for the diseases of old age, you may need to give extra attention to the following areas:

- **Diet**
  Many elderly cats are unable to chew their food as well as when they were younger and may need a softer diet. Your vet can advise you about special diets.

- **Joints**
  Although arthritis is not as common in cats as in many other species, elderly cats will often become less able to climb, and may need helping up onto their favourite spots.

- **Claws**
  If elderly cats stop scratching properly, their nails may need regular clipping.

- **Skin**
  Shorthaired cats may need additional grooming as they get older, and extra dietary supplements may help their coat condition.

Overgrown claws will need clipping.

- Older cats commonly get a heavy accumulation of soft tartar and harder calculus deposits on their teeth. This is a problem only when the gums become inflamed, which then leads to recession of the gums and infection around the roots.

- Any anaesthetic carries a slight risk, and that risk does get slightly greater as the patient gets older; but with modern anaesthetics the risks are still small in a healthy elderly cat, and they outweigh the risks of leaving an infected mouth untreated.

- I am sure your vet would be advising the procedure only if the problem really requires treating and if your cat is not suffering from any other condition that would rule out an anaesthetic.

MY VET WANTS TO ANAESTHETISE MY 16-YEAR-OLD CAT TO CLEAN HER TEETH. IS IT SAFE TO GO AHEAD?

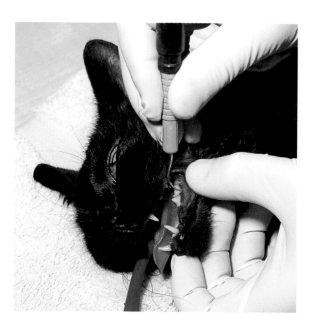

MY CAT HAS GONE BLIND. IS HE LIKELY TO BE ABLE TO COPE?

- It depends. Whereas dogs use their sense of smell as much as vision to guide themselves around, cats are much more dependent on their eyesight.

- If a cat goes blind very gradually, perhaps with cataracts, they may learn to adapt. A lot of owners do find that such cats can cope adequately provided they are kept indoors and the furniture is not moved around too often.

- It is not uncommon for elderly cats to go blind suddenly—for example because of detached retinas resulting from some underlying disease problem. This usually causes considerable distress and confusion, and most owners would choose to have their cat put to sleep in those circumstances.

LUCKY
MY LITTLE BABY
& SPECIAL FRIEND
1988 – 1997

WHAT HAPPENS TO MY CAT AFTER HE IS PUT TO SLEEP?

- This depends upon your vet, and you should discuss this matter with him or her beforehand if possible.
- Most clinics have arrangements with a pet crematorium, and you may be able, if you wish, to have your cat individually cremated and its ashes returned to you.
- Some people prefer to bury their pet on their own property or make arrangements with a pet cemetery.

MY CAT IS OLD AND INFIRM. SHOULD I HAVE HER PUT TO SLEEP OR LET HER DIE AT HOME?

- Most of us wish that our sick or elderly pets would just die peacefully in their sleep and spare us the heartache of having to make the decision to have them put to sleep. Unfortunately, life and death are not often like that, and many animals go through a period of suffering before they die.
- If a cat is very elderly or terminally ill and obviously not enjoying a good quality of life, it is kindest to allow your pet to end its days quickly and peacefully with a painless injection administered by a vet. This is a stronger version of a drug that can be used as an anaesthetic, and the cat literally 'goes to sleep'.

MY CAT DIED SEVERAL MONTHS AGO, AND YET I STILL GET VERY UPSET JUST THINKING ABOUT IT. IS THIS NORMAL?

- The important thing to appreciate is that it is very common for owners to feel deeply bereaved after the loss of a pet, because it has become a close member of the family.
- Many people are reluctant to admit this feeling or to discuss it with anyone, because they fear being ridiculed. If you are to get over the bereavement, you first have to face up to your feelings.
- It is also normal for owners to feel emotions such as guilt ('Could I have done more to save her?') or anger ('Why did the vet allow him to die?').
- However, these feelings, as well as depression and deep sorrow, should gradually be replaced by an acceptance of the cat's death and a more positive focusing on the happy years that it shared with you.
- Pet bereavement counsellors are available to help owners get through the experience of losing a pet. Your veterinary clinic should be able to put you in touch with a counsellor in your area.

The importance of a well-balanced diet is now established, and evidence suggests that domestic cats are enjoying an increasing life expectancy that is partly due to an improved standard of nutrition. For comparison we can look at feral cat colonies. Their food supply is a critical factor in the size and health of the group, and usually their diet consists mainly of rodents and, to a lesser extent, birds and food scavenged from human sources, such as dustbins. Although the physiology of the cat is

4 Diet

well adapted to obtaining all its nutritional needs from animal sources, the diet of feral cats is poor, resulting in a low life expectancy. The cat is increasingly being treated as part of the family, and some owners express their devotion to their cat by providing it with the most luxurious foods. An increasing number of products in the cat food market are high cost, attractively packaged foods with exotic ingredients. The most expensive is not necessarily the best, and if you allow your cat to dictate what it will eat, its diet may be unbalanced. The nutritional requirements of a cat are not static, they vary depending upon the stage of development in that animal's life, its level of activity, disease entities, and variation from one individual to another. Premium-quality life stage diets have been developed with differing energy densities, and different levels of protein, fat, and carbohydrate. The veterinary profession plays a role in advising cat owners on the best way to feed their cat at every stage in its development.

food facts

Feeding habits and problems, as well as ways to help fat cats lose weight.

HOW OFTEN SHOULD I FEED MY CAT?

- There is some difference of opinion about this. Some people prefer to feed their cat regular meals, getting into a routine of feeding an adult cat two or three times a day (more often for a kitten). Other people choose to leave food available all the time and allow the cat to eat as it pleases. This is more satisfactory with dry cat food, since it will not spoil if left out, even in hot weather.

- My preference is to feed cats whenever you wish. They are generally very good at adjusting their food intake to meet their needs, and a food can be selected with a calorie content best suited to the requirement of that cat. For example, if the cat is gaining weight, a lower-calorie food can be provided. However, this system breaks down in a multi-cat household where the cats have different requirements, and they will have to be fed separately.

HOW CAN I TELL IF MY CAT IS OVERWEIGHT?

- The normal weight for a cat can vary considerably, although most adults should weigh between 3.5 and 4.5kg (8–11 pounds) depending on breed, age and gender.

- More significant than absolute weight is the change in weight over a period of time, because if an adult cat is at a stable weight for a length of time and then starts either gaining or losing weight conspicuously, this could indicate a problem.

- Your vet will be able to look at your cat and let you know if it is the correct weight for its age, sex and breed.

- Yes. Although cats are not prone to coronary heart disease, which is a major problem in overweight humans—nor likely to be crippled by arthritis, which is particularly common in older overweight dogs, recent work has shown that life expectancy is significantly lower in overweight cats compared to those with a normal body weight.
- Liver disease and, particularly, diabetes mellitus are more common in overweight cats.

IS IT HARMFUL FOR A CAT TO BE OVERWEIGHT?

HOW CAN I GET SOME WEIGHT OFF MY RATHER TUBBY CAT?

- The first step is to recognise the importance of weight control and the need to do something about it for your pet, because there is little hope of success unless you take a positive attitude. It's very difficult to get a cat to do more exercise than it chooses, so the key must be reducing the cat's caloric intake.
- Dry catfoods are particularly high in calories, and should be stopped or replaced with a special low-calorie version.
- If you have more than one cat, and only one is overweight, you will have to work out a way of feeding them separately.
- You should speak to your vet about the best weight-reduction diet for your cat. Various products are available, but your cat should have a health examination to ensure that there is no underlying disease problem.
- Many clinics now run weight-reduction programmes to help pet owners get their pet's weight down, and regular weighing and guidance are useful in making sure that the correct procedure is being followed.
- Any change to a new diet should be carried out gradually, to avoid upsetting the cat's digestion and to encourage it to eat the new food. Warming a new diet or adding tiny amounts of liver or kidney juice can help to make a new diet more palatable. Starvation can cause serious liver problems, so it is better to find a low-calorie alternative. Aim for a gradual reduction over weeks or months to reach your cat's target weight, and then a change to a long-term diet to maintain the weight loss.

- Don't worry if your kitten doesn't want to drink, provided that he seems well and is eating food normally. Being descended from wild cats who lived in semi-desert lands, today's domestic cat is extremely efficient at conserving fluids.

- If you are feeding tinned or fresh food, it will contain quite a lot of moisture, and the metabolism of that food within the body produces more water, so that some cats hardly feel the need to drink at all. Whereas there are several diseases, such as kidney disease, diabetes, and hyperthyroidism that cause an increase in thirst, none are indicated by a decrease in thirst (except where this is part of a refusal to take anything by mouth).

- Make sure that fresh water is available to your kitten at all times, but don't try to coerce him to drink it.

HOW CAN I ENCOURAGE MY KITTEN TO DRINK MORE?

- Yes, providing that you do not suddenly stop again, because in time the cats will become dependent on your food source. You should also contact your local cat welfare organization to see if they will take responsibility for management of the colony.

- Current thinking suggests that the best control policy is to trap, neuter and release adults back onto the site and re-home small kittens. Neutered cats are marked while under anaesthetic, usually by removing the tip of one ear, so that any new additions to the colony can be readily identified and trapped.

I HAVE A COLONY OF FERAL CATS NEAR MY HOME. IS IT OK FOR ME TO FEED THEM?

HOW CAN I PREVENT MY CAT FROM GETTING CONSTIPATED?

- Be careful with the long-term use of laxatives such as mineral oil (liquid paraffin), for although they are not toxic, they can take the fat-soluble vitamins out of the bowel and eventually cause deficiencies to develop. Wheat bran added to the food in excessive amounts can also interfere with the absorption of other nutrients.

- A better alternative is one of the veterinary faecal consistency modifers (granules that absorb moisture into the bowel to soften the stools), which are given with the food and are safe for long-term use. Giving petroleum jelly on an intermittent basis will usually control hair balls and constipation.

- Regular grooming lessens the amount of dead hair swallowed and reduces constipation, as the hair binds the faeces together.

WHY DO CATS EAT GRASS?

- We don't really know, but many cats seem to regularly enjoy eating it.
- There is some suggestion that they tend to eat grass to make themselves vomit when they have a digestive upset, but this is unproven.
- The most likely explanation is that they have a natural instinct to eat grass to take in minute amounts of folic acid. This is needed in their bodies, but is not found in animal tissues. In the wild, cats may ingest enough folic acid by eating some of the stomach contents of their prey.
- It is a good idea to provide indoor cats with a tray of growing grass such as wheat or oat grass for them to fulfill their need if they wish, but keep away from the coarser ornamental grasses which can get stuck at the back of the throat or build up in the stomach or intestines.

MY CAT CHEWS ON HOUSEPLANTS. CAN THIS BE DANGEROUS?

- Yes. Quite a number of indoor plants can be toxic to cats; these include
- poinsettia
- Christmas cherry
- ivy
- spotted dieffenbachia (dumb cane)
- azalea
- You may need to put plants out of reach, or stay on guard and use some form of punishment such as a water spray if you catch your cat in the act.
- Many cats seem to feel the need to chew on some greenery, so if your cat lives indoors, you should provide an alternative in the form of a tray of oat or wheat grass.

which food?

Dietary requirements for health and the best cat foods for your pet.

ARE FRESH MEAT AND FISH BEST FOR CATS?

- Fresh meat and fish will not provide a balanced diet for your cat, as they are very high in protein and low in other important nutrients, especially calcium.
- While it is true that cats are carnivores and that in the wild they eat almost exclusively animal tissue, in that environment they will normally eat a whole carcass, including the internal organs, bones and stomach contents, which provide many nutrients that are not present in lean muscle tissue.
- It is possible to rear and maintain cats successfully on a fresh food diet, but you need to be very careful to add a variety of other foods to ensure that a complete diet is being fed.

CAN I FEED MY CAT ON A VEGETARIAN DIET?

- No. Whereas we humans, and even dogs, are able to manufacture within our bodies all the nutrients we need from a good-quality vegetarian diet, the cat is such a specialised hunter that during its evolution it has lost this ability.
- A deficiency of the amino acid taurine, an essential building block for proteins in the body, can cause both blindness and heart failure. Moreover, severe loss of condition and skin problems can be caused by a deficiency of certain essential fatty acids found only in animal flesh.
- By all means stick to a vegetarian diet for yourself; but if you are to keep a cat, you must accept that they are born carnivores.
- You may find a complete dry diet more aesthetically acceptable to handle than tinned or fresh meat.

IS IT OK TO GIVE A CAT ONLY DRY FOOD?

- Yes—providing that you feed a premium-quality dry food and always make sure that a supply of fresh water is available for your cat at all times.
- Several years ago, some link between dry diets and urinary tract disease was established in cats, but it was subsequently discovered that this was due to a problem with the make-up of the dry foods at that time and not that they were dry. This has now been corrected; in fact, special dry foods are sometimes prescribed to help in the treatment of cats that are suffering from urinary disease.
- Dry food is more convenient, more hygienic, and generally less expensive than tinned or fresh foods. It also exercises the teeth and reduces the buildup of tartar, which can become a major problem in cats fed on a soft and mushy diet.

- Yes. There are some foods that are so unbalanced that they can cause serious disease problems if eaten to excess. Examples of such problems include the following conditions:
- *Hypervitaminosis A*, caused by excessive amounts of vitamin A found in raw liver, producing a severe disorder of bone growth.
- *Thiamin deficiency*, caused by a diet of raw fish or raw eggs, both of which contain an enzyme that breaks down thiamin, an essential B vitamin. A deficiency of this vitamin will cause a severe nervous disorder.
- *Pansteatitis*, or yellow fat disease, is also caused by a diet based primarily on fish, especially red tuna. The disease is characterised by painful nodular swellings of the fatty tissue under the skin, and vitamin E deficiency.

ARE THERE ANY CAT FOODS THAT CAN BE HARMFUL TO MY CAT?

I FEED MY CAT ON TINNED FOOD. SHOULD I ALSO GIVE A VITAMIN AND MINERAL SUPPLEMENT?

- No. There is a common misconception that if vitamins and minerals are good, more of them must be even better, but this is not the case.
- Excessive amounts of certain vitamins or minerals can cause serious problems, and if you are feeding a good-quality complete cat food, it will contain the optimum balance of both.
- Generally, high-quality tinned food is more expensive. Ask your vet to recommend a suitable brand.

SHOULD I GIVE MY CAT MILK TO DRINK?

- Cats don't need milk in their diet, although many enjoy it. They cannot digest lactose (milk sugar) properly, and undigested lactose will tend to ferment in the lower bowel and cause diarrhoea.
- If your cat really enjoys milk and does not seem to suffer from any digestive upsets, you can give a limited amount—or, better still, give your cat one of the special cat milks from which the lactose has been removed.

MY CAT LIKES EATING DOG FOOD WITH MY DOG. SHOULD THIS BE HAPPENING?

- No. It's strange that dogs seem to like cat foods and cats often prefer to eat what the dog has in its bowl, but the makeup of these foods is very different.
- Cat food is too high in protein for dogs, so is not ideal in the long term, but dog food can be positively harmful to cats if fed for an extended period, notably leading to problems related to taurine deficiency.

special needs

Dietary-related conditions and how to alleviate them by offering special diets.

MY CAT KEEPS GETTING SKIN PROBLEMS. IS IT POSSIBLE THAT SHE IS ALLERGIC TO SOMETHING IN HER DIET?

- Yes, sometimes, depending upon what these stones are made of.
- Large stones sometimes form, but it is much more common for cats just to produce crystals in their urine; these tend to irritate the bladder and cause cystitis. In male cats these crystals can cause a blockage to the flow of urine from the bladder, so a male cat that is straining to urinate must receive immediate veterinary attention.

MY VET SAYS THAT A SPECIAL DIET CAN DISSOLVE BLADDER STONES. CAN THIS BE TRUE?

- The most common form of crystal is called struvite. These crystals consist mainly of magnesium compounds and tend to form when the urine is alkaline.
- Special diets that are low in magnesium and encourage the production of an acidic urine will help to dissolve the crystals, and may even dissolve a bladder stone that has formed.
- If the stones are causing acute distress or do not respond to medical treatment, they may need to be removed by surgery.

- An allergic reaction to something in the diet can cause skin disease, especially irritation around the head and neck region, although an allergic reaction to flea bites is more common and should be ruled out first.
- Skin problems may be caused by parasites, such as ringworm or ear mites. They can also cause skin irritation and scratching. Roundworms also often cause allergies.
- The most common reactions are to proteins, but not only those found in meat—reactions to substances such as wheat or milk proteins have also been found. It is not necessary for the cat to have had a change of diet just before the onset of the skin problem. Allergies can develop after a food has been fed for some time.
- The only sure way to tell is to put the cat on a special low-allergy diet for at least four weeks and monitor the effects.
- Several commercial preparations are available, and your vet will be able to select one that is most likely to be effective for your cat. If you have a cat on a low-allergy food, you must feed the diet exclusively for the test period, which will mean keeping the cat indoors to prevent scavenging.

Female cat in homemade collar and pyjamas to prevent her from scratching an allergic skin complaint.

WHAT IS THE BEST DIET FOR MY DIABETIC CAT?

● Diabetes mellitus (sugar diabetes) is very closely linked to obesity in cats, and some mildly diabetic cats can be treated simply by feeding a reduced-calorie diet to bring their weight down to within the normal range.

● Very little research has been carried out to identify the best diet for cats that are receiving insulin therapy, but we do know that the metabolism of the cat is very different from that of the dog or the human, and we cannot assume that what applies to those species will apply to the cat.

● The most important dietary consideration is to feed a constant diet, without undue variation in calorie intake from one day to the next; otherwise insulin requirements will fluctuate wildly.

● The ideal is probably a diet that is moderately restricted in calories, with higher levels of soluble fibre from fruits, oats, beans, peas and lentils to slow down the absorption of carbohydrates from the bowel.

MY CAT HAS HAD SEVERAL TEETH REMOVED. WILL SHE BE ABLE TO EAT HER FOOD?

● It's surprising how well cats can manage without their teeth if they have to, and some cats without any teeth at all seem able to cope even with dry food.

● Her teeth may have been removed because of painful abscesses. These can be a cause of kidney failure and heart disease and you will probably find that her eating will be better rather than worse.

● Avoid changing from one food to another. Some cats seem unable to digest certain brands of tinned food; others tend to vomit on dry foods, so you should find out what suits your cat and stick to it.

● If you suspect that your cat's digestive problems may relate to her diet, I suggest you feed a diet of fresh white meat or fish, preferably mixed with a little rice and a balanced vitamin and mineral supplement for a three-week trial period.

● If her problems settle down, you then know it was her previous diet that was causing her problem, and you can gradually add one thing at a time to her diet to see what she can and can't digest.

MY CAT IS PRONE TO VOMITING. WHAT DIET IS BEST FOR HER?

SHOULD I WORRY IF MY CAT DOESN'T EAT FOR A DAY OR TWO?

● It depends upon your cat's normal habits. You will be familiar with your own cat's routine and know if he never misses a meal or if he's the type of cat that sometimes doesn't bother with his food.

● If a cat is otherwise well but does not eat for a couple of days, don't be immediately concerned. He may be eating elsewhere.

● If the cat seems ill, or refuses to eat for longer than 48 hours, it's time to seek veterinary advice.

- We have only recently begun to understand the dietary needs of older cats. Whereas elderly dogs tend to put on weight because they become less active, elderly cats usually become markedly less efficient at absorbing and digesting their food. This means that they usually need a higher-energy diet rather than a low-calorie option.
- Cats with specific diseases common in old age, such as kidney disease, will need specific diets to control that particular problem.

ARE THERE ANY SPECIAL DIETARY NEEDS FOR ELDERLY CATS?

- Worms often get the blame for all sorts of problems, but it is unusual for them to cause illness in adult cats. Take a stool sample to the vet in case he or she wants to perform a faecal analysis to rule out the existence of internal parasites. The symptoms could also be those of a hyperadrenal cat.
- There are other specific disease problems that can cause excessive eating and weight loss in older cats. These include an overactive thyroid gland, chronic diarrhoea, diabetes mellitus and certain cancerous growths, in which a rapidly growing tumour burns up energy and deprives the cat.
- Take your cat to your vet for a checkup and blood tests.

MY ELDERLY CAT NOW EATS A LOT MORE FOOD BUT IS LOSING WEIGHT. IS THIS DUE TO WORMS?

- Getting a cat to change to a diet that is best for him, instead of one he considers the tastiest, can be very difficult, especially when the cat is not feeling well anyway.
- You should make any changes gradually, mixing increasing amounts of the new food in with the old, until you are feeding the new one exclusively (see page 58).
- Hand feeding the food or slightly warming it may also increase its appeal.
- A change of diet can significantly improve the life expectancy of a cat with kidney disease, so it is well worth persevering.

MY CAT HAS A SPECIAL DIET FOR KIDNEY DISEASE. HOW CAN I GET HIM TO REALISE THAT HE HAS TO EAT IT?

A cat's coat is one of its most striking and appealing features. However, the skin and coat also perform some very important functions:

Protection from injury and infection: The skin of the tom-cat is tough to serve as protection when the cat fights to defend its territory. Extra-thick skin over his cheeks gives him a distinctive appearance not seen in a neutered male.

Heat regulation: The coat provides insulation against cold weather and protects the skin against the effects of ultraviolet radiation.

5 Grooming

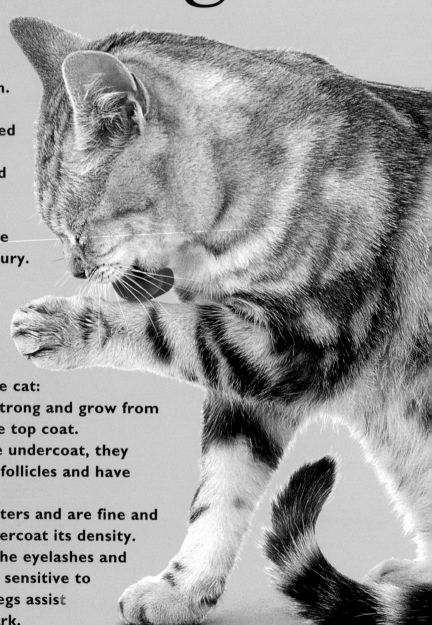

Water conservation: The outer skin is waterproof, and a cat that loses much of its skin will die from dehydration.

Sense of touch: This is dependent upon sensors buried within the skin that transmit information to the spinal cord and then to the brain. Pain sensors transmit unpleasant sensations but play a vital role in protecting the cat from injury.

Camouflage: A tabby colouration is good camouflage in woods, and black town cats can blend into dark alleyways.

Three types of hairs cover the cat:

Guard hairs are long and strong and grow from individual follicles to form the top coat.

Awn hairs form part of the undercoat, they emerge in clusters from hair follicles and have thickened, bristle-like tips.

Down hairs emerge in clusters and are fine and woolly, and help give the undercoat its density.

Specialised hairs, such as the eyelashes and the *vibrissae*, or whiskers, are sensitive to touch. Whiskers on the forelegs assist their sense of touch in the dark.

grooming routine

How to groom, bathe and take care of your cat's eyes, ears and claws.

WHY DO CATS
GROOM
THEMSELVES?

- Cats are fastidious creatures and normally will spend a lot of time maintaining their coat in good condition.
- You will quickly notice if your cat stops grooming, as the coat soon loses its normal luster, becoming dull and matted.

**WHY HAS MY
CAT STOPPED
GROOMING
HERSELF?**

- This may indicate that the cat is feeling generally ill; but it is much more likely to be a sign that the cat is suffering from a specific problem that makes grooming painful. For example, sore gums, an ulcer on the tongue, or even arthritis in the vertebrae of the neck may all make grooming uncomfortable.
- When a sick cat starts to groom itself again, this is a sure sign that things are looking up and the patient is once more starting to take an interest in life.

- The primary aim is to keep the coat in good order. Cats have a grooming routine that enables them to get at almost every part of their body with their tongue, which is equipped with comb-like spines to help in the process. The few bits around the head and ears that cannot be reached with the tongue are cleaned with the inner dew claw, which is licked and then pulled through the coat.
- Besides removing dead hairs, sloughed skin cells and any parasites, the massaging action of the tongue stimulates the skin glands to produce a light film of oil which has the effect of waterproofing the skin.
- Grooming also performs two other important functions.
- First, unlike some other mammals, the cat does not sweat from most of its body surface area, and the evaporation of saliva from the coat performs a similar function, helping to keep it cool in warm weather.
- Second, where two or more cats share a home, mutual grooming plays an important social bonding role between them, particularly between a female and her young. It also helps to deal with those really hard-to-get-to spots!

- If your cat has a coat that needs grooming, it is best to get into the habit of doing it every day.
- Don't rush the procedure; let it be a pleasurable experience for both you and the cat, strengthening the bond between you, just as mutual grooming does among cats.
- Once you allow knots to form in the coat, the whole process becomes a painful struggle for both cat and owner.

WHAT IMPLEMENTS DO I NEED FOR GROOMING MY CAT?

- The most important tool for grooming your cat is a fine-toothed comb. Often described as flea combs, these are actually of little use for flea control but are excellent for getting right down to the depths of the coat and removing all the dead hair. For a cat with a thick, long coat, you may need to use a coarser comb.
- A brush with metal bristles embedded into a rubber base is also useful.
- Many cats enjoy a massage with a grooming mitt, which has rubber spikes on the palm to remove dead hairs.
- Any knots that cannot be teased out will need to be cut out, using a pair of 'curved on flat' scissors. These have blunt ends and curved blades to reduce the chance of nicking the skin.
- You may also need a supply of cotton buds, cotton wool, talcum powder for Persians, a toothbrush, nail clippers and a chamois leather or rubber brush for a shorthaired cat.

- The key to successful grooming is to start young so that your cat gets used to the experience as early as possible and eventually looks forward to it.
- Grooming also needs to be carried out very regularly, before any serious knots form, because once the coat becomes matted, the grooming process becomes painful and the cat starts to object. The owner then has to use force to achieve what is necessary, and it is not surprising that the next time grooming is attempted the cat does all it can to avoid a repeat performance.

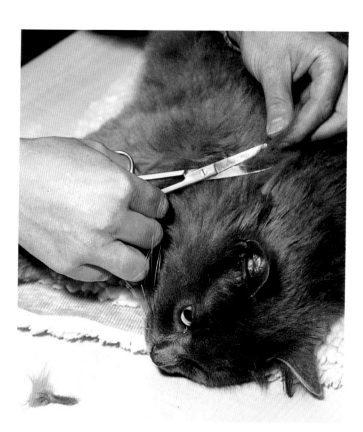

MY CAT GETS REALLY AGGRESSIVE WHEN I TRY TO GROOM HIM. HOW CAN I COPE?

- Once you have got into a confrontational situation when grooming your cat, it's very difficult to return to an even keel. You may be able to resolve the problem simply by teasing or cutting out the knots just a few at a time, particularly when your cat is sleepy and relaxed.
- If the problem is advanced, it may be better to arrange for your vet to de-mat your cat under sedation, and for you then to start grooming regularly before knots have a chance to re-form.

WHEN DOES A CAT NEED TO BE GROOMED MOST OFTEN?

- Many cats, such as the Angora, develop a thick coat in winter, and this is shed when the weather gets warmer. Therefore, grooming for these breeds is most important during the moulting season in the spring.
- Cats that live a sheltered indoor life all year round will shed their coat in dribs and drabs throughout the year.

WILL GROOMING PREVENT MY CAT FROM GETTING HAIRBALLS?

- Because the spines on a cat's tongue point in down toward the throat, cats will tend to swallow a great deal of dead hair while they are grooming.
- This is not usually a problem, as the hair usually just passes out of the digestive system, but the hair can build up in the stomach to form what is known as a hairball. Sometimes these hairballs are vomited up, which solves the problem, but other times the cat is unable to clear them, and either retches repeatedly or stops eating because the stomach feels distended.
- Excessive amounts of swallowed hair may also aggravate constipation in cats that are prone to this problem. Laxatives such as mineral oil will help the hair to pass through, but should not be used frequently as they can interfere with the absorption of fat-soluble vitamins.
- Regular grooming will certainly help to reduce the amount of dead hair that is ingested and thus lower the incidence of these related problems.

coat care

Step-by-step grooming, bathing and caring for your cat's coat.

WHAT IS THE BEST WAY TO GROOM A LONGHAIRED CAT?

- First gently comb out the hair thoroughly to untangle any knots, starting on the abdomen and legs, then combing along the back against the lie of the coat, and finally comb the fur in an upward direction around the neck to form a ruff.
- A little talcum powder sprinkled onto the coat will help to remove grease and dirt and make it easier to tease out any tangles.
- Then vigorously brush into the lie of the coat with a bristle brush, working from head to tail and removing all talcum powder from the coat.
- Finally, make a part down the middle of the tail and gently brush the fur out to each side.

DO DIFFERENT TYPES OF CAT HAVE DIFFERING HAIR TYPES?

- Yes. The overall length and proportion of hairs will vary from breed to breed, with longhaired cats such as Persians having very long down hairs which are nearly the same length as the guard hairs, whereas in other longhaired breeds, such as the Angora, the guard hairs are much longer, giving a silkier coat.
- The Rex cats have very strange coats that are generally short and curly. The Selkirk Rex originated in Wyoming in 1987 and has a thick curly coat. The Cornish Rex lacks guard hairs, and its curliness is due to the natural curl of the soft awn and down hairs. The Devon Rex has all three hair types, but all are modified, and the whiskers may be absent or just be fragile, crinkled stubs.
- The strangest coat of all belongs to the Sphynx, which appears to be completely bald, but actually has a covering of fine down hairs on some parts of its body.

WHAT ARE THE BLACK SPECKS IN MY CAT'S FUR?

- These are most likely flea dirt, droppings that are passed by fleas.
- The fleas themselves move very quickly and are difficult to spot, but flea dirt can be an important indication that flea treatment is necessary.
- You may notice it on the cat's bedding after it gets up. You can distinguish flea dirt from ordinary grit by putting a bit onto some damp cotton wool.
- Because flea dirt is composed mainly of dried blood, you will see a pinkish halo form around it.

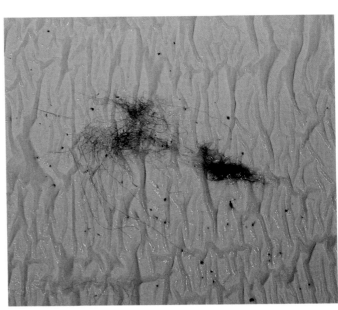

1 *Comb out hair along the abdomen and legs.*

2 *Comb along back against the lie of the coat.*

3 *Comb around the neck to form a ruff.*

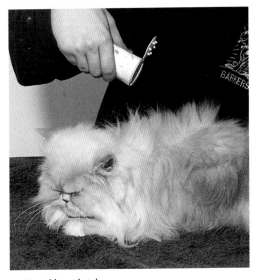

4 *Sprinkle with talc.*

5 *Brush into lie of coat from head to tail.*

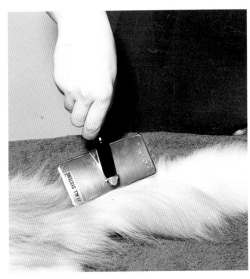

6 *Brush tail out to each side.*

DO I NEED TO GROOM A SHORTHAIRED CAT?

- Many shorthaired cats are perfectly able to look after their coats by themselves, but not all cats seem to manage as well as others, especially when they are ill or if they are elderly.
- A regular grooming session also gives the owner a chance to give the cat a thorough physical checking-over, which may pick up problems such as skin parasites or ear infections before they become well established.
- If you plan to show your shorthaired cat, even in a nonpedigree class, you will need to get it used to regular grooming.
- A fine comb should be used to remove any knots, followed by a rubber brush or mitt, which will remove dead hair and skin cells without scratching the skin.
- A slightly dampened chamois cloth can be used to massage the skin and smooth down the coat, mimicking the action of the cat's tongue.

1 *Use a fine comb to remove any knots.*

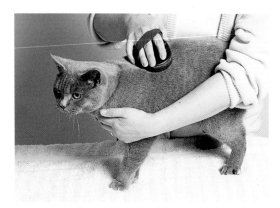

2 *A rubber brush is used to remove dead hair and skin cells.*

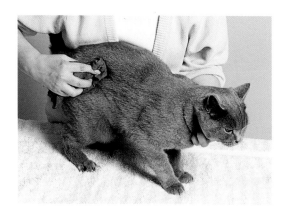

3 *Finally, a damp chamois cloth will smooth down the coat.*

SHOULD I EVER BATHE MY CAT?

- There is hardly ever a real necessity to bathe a cat, but show cats are bathed regularly, usually a few days before the show. You may be asked by your vet to give your cat a medicated shampoo to treat a specific skin condition. If you are allergic to cats, you may find that regular bathing (of your cat!) reduces your reaction.
- First, get everything ready that you are likely to need, because if your cat is not accustomed to being bathed, you will need all hands on deck to cope.
- Use a safe cat shampoo, a plastic bowl, a plastic jug, a soft cloth and a towel.
- Put about 10cm (4 inches) of warm water into the bowl and lift the cat firmly into the bath, holding it by its scruff.
- Wet the cat with a little shampoo mixed with warm water poured from the jug, massaging the shampoo well into the coat, working from the head backwards, and taking care not to get soap into the cat's eyes or ears.
- Rinse the cat thoroughly, using plenty of warm water poured from the jug or from a shower, and then lift the cat from the bath and into the towel to dry.
- Use the dampened soft cloth to wipe around the cat's eyes, ears and nose.
- Some cats will tolerate being dried off with a hairdryer, but make sure it's not too hot.

1 *Hold your cat firmly by the scruff and put it into the bath.*

2 *Massage the shampoo well into the coat.*

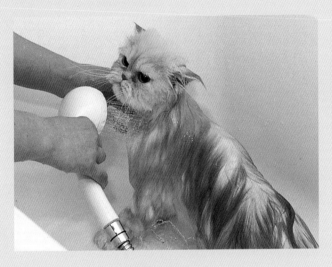

3 *Thoroughly rinse out the shampoo.*

4 *Lift your cat out of the bath and towel dry.*

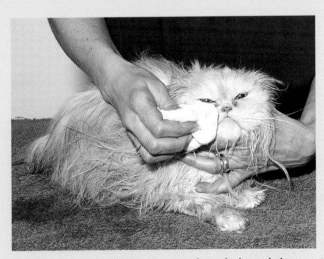

5 *Wipe the cat's eyes, ears and nose with a soft, damp cloth.*

6 *Use a hairdryer to finish drying off if your cat will tolerate this.*

- It is important that whatever you use is nontoxic to cats, for it will be groomed off and swallowed by the cat.
- I would not recommend the use of insecticidal shampoos for cats unless specifically prescribed by your vet, as there are many more effective ways of dealing with pests such as fleas and ticks.
  - Use a low-allergy shampoo specifically for cats.
  - Some people advocate the use of warm bran rubbed into the coat of shorthaired cats as a dry shampoo to help remove grease and dirt from the coat.

WHAT IS THE BEST SHAMPOO TO USE ON MY CAT?

- It's not uncommon for cats to suffer from dandruff, which is due to an excessive shedding of dead skin cells.
- If mild, it may be of little significance, but it should receive attention if it is severe or if the skin looks inflamed.
- Many cats do not absorb essential fatty acids from their diet very well, and a dietary supplement that contains trace elements such as zinc, vitamins such as vitamin A, and essential fatty acids will often help a great deal. Gamma linolenic acid (GLA) is particularly useful and is present in large amounts in evening primrose oil.
- Dandruff may also be caused by skin irritation, most commonly caused by parasites such as fleas, or 'walking dandruff'— a tiny mite with the scientific name of *cheyletiella* that is not uncommon in longhaired cats.

WHY DOES MY CAT HAVE SO MUCH DANDRUFF?

- It is important to remove any harmful substance, such as paint or varnish, that contaminates a cat's coat, to prevent it from irritating the skin or being swallowed during the grooming process and poisoning the cat.
  - In removing the substance, avoid using any solvents that may be toxic.
  - You may be able to remove some of the substance by clipping the hair short, since it will tend to affect the most superficial layers of the coat. You can use a liquid soap, or a gel-based hand cleaner.
- In cases of severe contamination, seek veterinary assistance quickly.

MY CAT HAS GOT PAINT OR VARNISH ON ITS COAT. HOW CAN I GET IT OFF?

Wrap your cat securely in a towel so that you have one hand free to clean its coat

finishing touches

How to complete your cat's grooming routine and keep him in good condition.

SHOULD I CLEAN MY CAT'S EARS REGULARLY?

- A healthy cat's ears should not accumulate excessive amounts of wax and should not need cleaning.
- Discharge from the ears may be a sign of an ear infection, and any appearance of black crumbly wax may indicate that the cat has an ear mite infestation.
- If you have had your cat's ears checked by a vet and are confident that regular cleaning is all that is needed, you should use a small amount of warm olive oil, or a commercial feline ear cleaner.
- Do not poke any cleaning sticks down into the ear, but simply instil a few drops while holding the ear flap firmly to stop the cat from shaking its head, then massage the oil well down into the ear canal.
- Use cotton wool to wipe away any of the oil and wax that come to the surface.

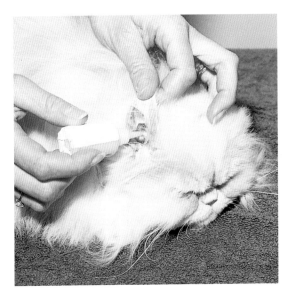

1 *Instil a few drops of oil into your cat's ear.*

2 *Massage the oil well into the ear canal.*

3 *Wipe away any oil and wax that appears.*

HOW DO I CLEAN MY CAT'S EYES?

● A discharge from the eyes could be a sign of a medical problem that requires veterinary attention, particularly if it is thick and yellow, or if the eyes look sore.

● Persians are especially prone to runny eyes because the shape of their face may interfere with the drainage of tears from the eyes. Cats that have suffered a serious bout of cat flu may also be left with a chronically discharging eye that requires regular cleaning.

● If it is left for too long, the discharge may cake into a hard mass that is very difficult to remove.

● Use cotton wool moistened with warm water, and wipe carefully, keeping away from the surface of the eye itself.

● A little petroleum jelly can be applied to the area to prevent the skin in the corner of the eyes becoming sore.

ARE THERE ANY PRODUCTS FOR CLEANING MY CAT'S TEETH?

● Yes, there are enzymatic toothpastes specifically designed for use with cats.

● Don't use human toothpaste, which would cause your cat to froth at the mouth and could be harmful if swallowed.

● Not many owners are able to cope with brushing their cat's teeth, but dental problems are very common and the effort is well worthwhile.

● Start a regular dental routine when your cat is young, and initially use a finger toothbrush, which fits over a finger, or just a piece of gauze wrapped around your finger.

● Don't assume that you can wait until after your kitten has lost its temporary teeth at around five months of age; if you do not start when your cat is young, you will have little chance of success.

IS THERE ANYTHING ELSE I CAN DO TO KEEP MY CAT'S TEETH IN GOOD CONDITION?

- Yes. Research has shown that tartar builds up significantly less quickly on the teeth of cats fed a diet of dry cat food, and there are now special fibrous dry cat foods designed to reduce tartar accumulation even further.
- It is even possible to buy chews for cats, and surprisingly enough, many cats do seem willing to chew on them.
- If the gums are significantly inflamed, it may be necessary for your vet to de-scale them under an anaesthetic.

CAN I CUT MY CAT'S CLAWS?

- You can do this, but they are best left uncut if at all possible.
- The claw is composed of multiple layers of horny tissue, somewhat like the skin of an onion, and when the outer layer becomes frayed and blunt, it is shed to leave a fresh nail underneath. The cat bites off the outer nail or pulls it off on a scratching post.
- Cutting off the points of the nails interferes with this natural shedding process, but is sometimes necessary in elderly cats that are too frail to scratch normally, with the result that the nails overgrow to the point where they can actually grow back around into the toe itself.
- It is also common practice to clip the nails of show cats to prevent them from scratching the judges, but only the very tips of the nails are removed.
- Special claw clippers should be used, and the sensitive quick, which is pink due to its blood supply, should be avoided; this can be clearly seen by viewing the claw against the light.

SHOULD CATS BE DE-CLAWED?

- In the United Kingdom and other countries it is considered unethical for vets to de-claw cats. However, in the United States cats are often de-clawed to prevent them from damaging furnishings.
- Cats that roam outdoors need their claws for climbing and for defense.
- The severity of the surgical operation involved should not be underestimated, since the cat's nails have to be cut away right down to the bone to prevent them from re-growing.
- It is almost always possible to re-direct the cat's normal scratching behaviour to a site where it does no harm, and the operation should be considered only as a last resort, as an alternative to euthanasia.

A Foreign Lilac cat sharpening her claws on a dead branch (above). The outer sheath of a cat's claw stuck in bark after a scratching session (above left).

Prevention is better than cure. Many steps can be taken to ensure that a cat has a long and healthy life, starting with a well-bred, sturdy kitten and continuing with regular veterinary preventive health care such as vaccinations, annual health checks and worming. A healthy lifestyle will increase a cat's chance of shrugging off disease when it threatens, and its immune system is normally able to offer protection from potentially harmful organisms. We shall see in a later chapter that a high-quality diet is also very important in maintaining good health, and feeding a cat what it chooses to eat does not always provide it with the nutrients it needs.

6 Health & Diseases

Even with the very best of care, disease will strike sooner or later. Look for any change in your cat's normal pattern of behaviour. This can be difficult with an outdoor cat; for example, a chronic case of diarrhoea may go unnoticed because the cat urinates and defecates outdoors. If a disease is detected early and treated before the problem becomes serious, the cat has a greater chance of surviving it.

Cat owners are often eager to treat problems at home, because of the expense of veterinary treatment. Care must be taken with using over-the-counter remedies, since they may be toxic to cats. This applies to topical applications such as aromatherapies, as they will be licked off the coat and swallowed. The main danger with most proprietary cures is not that they will harm the cat, but that they will fail to treat the disease. This will make a cure difficult and costly to achieve when professional help is sought.

vets

Choosing a vet and how to proceed when you have found someone suitable to look after your cat's health.

HOW CAN I FIND A GOOD VET?

- It's essential that you try to cultivate a long-term relationship of mutual trust with a vet or veterinary clinic in your area, and you should not make your selection according to price and convenience alone.

- You should be looking for a caring, friendly and well-trained staff, clean and well-maintained facilities, efficiently kept records and a full range of medical and surgical backup facilities.

- There are now many practices that specialise in treating cats, perhaps with a separate cat waiting area. You certainly want to ensure that your vet has an active interest in feline medicine.

- The best way to track down a good vet is by recommendation from other cat owners.

- Alternatively, you can look in the Yellow Pages or scan local newspaper advertisements. Especially in the latter case, you should consider arranging to go along to talk to the staff and view the facility before you register your cat.

- Most vets prefer to see cases at their clinics. This is because they have all the equipment and drugs on hand that they are likely to need, and it is much easier to check out a cat thoroughly on an examination table with proper lighting and nursing assistance.

- It is also much more time consuming to visit a cat in your home; if travelling time is taken into account, your vet could probably see five or six patients at the clinic in the same length of time, and this has to be reflected in the charge made to you.

- However, there are vets that make a point of making, or even encouraging, house visits. If you are still adamant that you want your cat examined in your home, and have discussed the matter with your vet, you may have to phone around to find a practice with a different policy on house calls.

MY VET DOES NOT MAKE HOUSE CALLS, BUT I HATE HAVING TO TAKE MY CAT TO THE CLINIC.

WHAT IF I AM UNHAPPY WITH THE CARE MY VET IS PROVIDING?

- Again, the first step should be to discuss it with your vet, and, if appropriate, with the senior partner of the practice. If you are still not satisfied with the treatment your pet is receiving, you should consider moving to another practice.

- It is very important that you notify the first clinic and arrange for them to forward your pet's clinical records to the new practice, so your new vet has all details of examinations carried out and treatment given.

- If you feel badly aggrieved about treatment and advice you have already received, you could make a malpractice complaint to the Royal College of Veterinary Surgeons. This governing body has disciplinary powers that they can use if they agree that the vet has acted in an unprofessional manner.

- You could also consider suing in the civil courts for negligence, but most vets have professional indemnity insurance, and unless a settlement is offered in a clear-cut case, you could face a long and costly legal battle.

WHAT IF I AM UNABLE TO AFFORD NORMAL VETERINARY FEES?

- Initially, you should discuss the matter with your own vet. Many practices are prepared to offer reduced fees or staggered payments to clients requiring a major course of treatment for their pet, provided they are satisfied that the need and the intention to pay are genuine. If you are not able to come to a satisfactory arrangement, you could contact one of the animal welfare organisations, who might be prepared to contribute towards the cost of treatment for your cat.

- The problem is best avoided, if possible. Owning a pet is not a necessity, and you should not take on the responsibility if you are not reasonably confident that you will be able to meet the likely costs—although, of course, people's circumstances may change.

- Pet health insurance plans are now available in many areas, and are generally an excellent way of insuring against any sudden unexpected expense and making sure your cat can get the very best treatment when it is needed.

general health

Often-asked questions relating to your cat's health and well being.

WHAT IS THE NORMAL BODY TEMPERATURE OF A CAT?

- There is some variation from one individual to another, but anything over 39°C (102°F) might be considered abnormal.
- This temperature is normally taken rectally, with either a special stubby-ended mercury thermometer or, preferably, an electronic thermometer, in which case there is no danger of it breaking accidentally.
- I would not advise the average cat owner to try to take his or her own cat's temperature. The sphincter muscles around the anus are very strong in the cat, and most cats, quite understandably, resent the procedure and struggle furiously.
- There is a danger that you will cause some damage to your cat, and it is a task that is best left to the experts.

HOW CAN I WEIGH MY CAT?

- You may be able to persuade your cat to sit still on bathroom scales. Alternatively, you can put your cat in its carrier, weigh them together, and then check and subtract the weight of the carrier.
- It is a good idea to weigh your cat on a regular basis to detect any long-term changes in body weight.

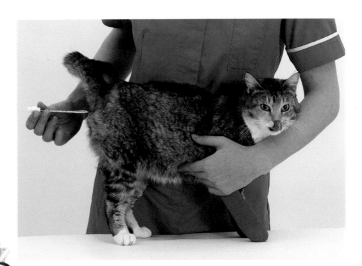

HOW LONG CAN A CAT SURVIVE WITHOUT EATING?

- One might think about ten minutes, judging by the frantic screams that we cat owners are subjected to when our cats want food and find an empty bowl!
- The truth is that cats can survive for several weeks without eating, and it is far more important in the short term that they take in fluids and do not get dehydrated.
- Very rarely, a cat that refuses to eat can develop a fatty degeneration of its liver, that can then become life threatening.

We humans become familiar with the normal behaviour patterns of our pet cats, and we can often sense that something is not quite right even if we are not sure exactly what it is. Obvious signs of illness include:

- Runny or sore eyes
- Discharge from the ears
- Loss of balance
- Loss of appetite
- Difficulty in swallowing
- Coughing
- Laboured breathing
- Excessive sneezing, possibly with a nasal discharge
- Lameness
- Matted coat
- Sores or abnormal swellings
- Vomiting
- Diarrhoea
- Some signs of ill health may be quite subtle so that they can be spotted only with close observation. For example, excessive thirst is a very common sign of ill health in older cats, but among cats who drink out-of-doors, this change might be detected only as a change in drinking pattern; for example, the cat begins regularly drinking from a garden pond if it never did so in the past. Similarly, a cat may have diarrhoea, but the only sign that the owner sees is some faecal staining around the anus, or perhaps just the cat grooming itself excessively in that area.

WHY DO CATS JUST HIDE AWAY WHEN THEY ARE ILL?

HOW WILL I KNOW WHEN MY CAT IS ILL?

- In the wild, a cat that is injured and unable to defend itself properly is likely to make a tasty meal for some other predator. It therefore makes great sense for an injured cat to drag itself away to a sheltered spot until it has regained its strength and can defend itself.
- It is not uncommon for a cat to disappear after being hit by a car and then turn up on the doorstep a few days later. The cat has a tremendously resilient body that is capable of recovering from even serious injuries with the minimum of assistance.

ARE FERAL CAT COLONIES A DISEASE HAZARD?

- There is no evidence that feral cat colonies pose a significant hazard to human health. However, from a feline point of view, many cats in a feral colony may be in very poor condition, and problems such as viral infections and parasitic infestations are more likely to be widespread.
- Many cat welfare organisations are running health programmes combined with population control efforts, as outlined on page 59, to vaccinate and worm cats when they are trapped.
- Cats that are severely diseased should be humanely destroyed to prevent them from suffering.
- Once the size of the colony has been regulated by neutering, additional feeding will do much to improve the physical condition of the cats.

general ailments

How to recognise normal behaviour as well as sickness in your cat.

- It is quite common for a cat to vomit from time to time to get rid of foreign matter in its stomach, such as hair or those little bits of mouse that are rather hard to digest. Some cats also vomit because they are not digesting their food properly; for example, some cats do not tolerate tinned foods, while others eat dry foods too quickly and tend to regurgitate them right after eating.
- Mild cases of vomiting may be corrected with a bland, low-fat diet, such as chicken or boiled white fish mixed with some white rice, fed little and often for at least two weeks.
- If the problem does not subside, and occurs frequently, you should contact your vet.
- Vomiting can also be a sign of a more serious problem, such as kidney failure, poisoning, or intestinal obstruction.
- If your cat is vomiting severely or bringing up blood, or is otherwise unwell, immediate veterinary attention is needed.

WHAT DOES IT MEAN IF MY CAT'S THIRD EYELIDS PROTRUDE OVER PART OF THE EYES?

- This condition of third eyelid protrusion, which is often accompanied by mild diarrhoea, has been recognised for many years, but its cause is unknown.
- Research now suggests that this is caused by a virus, called a torovirus, which temporarily paralyses the nerves controlling the third eyelid. Apart from diarrhoea, cats are not usually ill, and it resolves itself within a few weeks.
- No drugs, other than symptomatic treatment for the diarrhoea, are likely to help.
- A tumour behind the eye, a smaller-sized eye and any painful condition of the eye can also cause the protrusion of the third eyelid.

MY CAT HAS VERY LABOURED BREATHING. WHAT ARE THE LIKELY CAUSES?

- Laboured breathing, or dyspnea, is often a sign of a serious underlying illness in cats. Most commonly it results from an accumulation of fluid in the pleural cavity. This is normally only a very small space between the lungs and the chest wall, but it can fill up with fluid to the point where the lungs are floating within the chest, and eventually the cat is unable to breathe at all. Common causes include:

- **Tumours**
  Especially thymic lymphosarcoma, which is a cancer of the thymus gland in the chest, usually associated with feline leukaemia virus infection.
- **Diaphragmatic hernia**
  With a rupture in the diaphragm caused by some injury such as a road accident.
- **Pyothorax**
  An accumulation of pus caused by infection settling on the chest from a direct puncture wound, or via the bloodstream.
- **Feline infectious peritonitis**
- **Heart disease**
  Particularly in older cats.

- There are many possible causes of a chronic cough—such as chronic bronchitis, asthma, and lungworm infestation.
- Blood tests, an X-ray of the chest, and possibly an examination of washings taken from within the airways under anaesthetic will help a vet in reaching a diagnosis.
- Chronic bronchitis usually responds to a prolonged course of antibiotics, but asthma may require long-term suppression with anti-inflammatory drugs before it can be effectively controlled.

> **MY CAT GETS A VERY DRY COUGH, ESPECIALLY AT NIGHT. WHAT IS THE LIKELY CAUSE?**

> **WHY DOES MY CAT KEEP GETTING ULCERS ON HER UPPER LIP?**

- This is probably a rodent ulcer, also known as eosinophilic granulomas. This can occur on other parts of the body also and can be caused by fleas.
- The ulceration is caused by excessive grooming by the cat.
- Flea treatment is obviously necessary (see page 93), but some cases require long-term anti-inflammatory drugs.
- Use metal or ceramic dishes rather than plastic, which can harbour the bacteria that cause this condition.

- Chronic sinusitis most commonly follows a severe bout of cat flu and is due to secondary bacterial infection taking advantage of the damage to the lining of the nose. There are other causes, such as fungal infections, foreign bodies, and growths that can affect the throat or the nasal chambers and cause these symptoms.
- Your vet may want to X-ray your cat to see what the cause is, and possibly take swabs for culture to make sure that the right antibiotic is selected. If the cause is simply a chronic infection, a course of antibiotics may need to be given from time to time to keep infection under control.
- You may find that taking the cat into a steamy room, such as the bathroom when you take a bath, may help to loosen the mucus.

> **MY CAT HAS HAD A SNUFFLY NOSE FOR MONTHS. HOW CAN SHE GET RID OF IT?**

Birman with chronic rhinitis.

Taking a swab for culture from a cat's nose.

Your cat may be drinking more than you are aware of.

MY 15-YEAR-OLD CAT IS DRINKING A LOT. SHOULD I BE CONCERNED?

- Yes, unless the increase in thirst is caused by a reduced intake of water from other sources, such as when a cat goes onto a dry diet, or by an excessive loss of water, such as in extreme heat or if the cat is suffering from diarrhoea.
- Excessive thirst can be a key sign of several illnesses, particularly in elderly cats. These are:

- **Kidney disease**
  This is usually due to chronic scarring of the kidneys, but is sometimes caused by other factors, such as poisoning with ethylene glycol (antifreeze), which is deadly but which cats evidently find very tasty. Increased thirst is the first sign of a problem; the cat then begins to lose its appetite, and consequently loses weight. If the disease is identified early enough, a special diet will help to reduce the buildup of toxic waste products in the body and can result in a significant increase in life expectancy.

- **Hyperthyroidism**
  An overactivity of one or both of the thyroid glands in the neck is very common in older cats. Because these glands control the metabolic rate, affected cats will tend to be overactive, eat and drink more than usual, yet lose weight dramatically. If the condition is left untreated, the racing heart becomes unable to cope with the strain, and the cat will die from heart failure. Treatments include drugs, surgical removal of one or both glands, or radioactive iodine.

- **Diabetes mellitus (sugar diabetes)**
  This is due to a decreased production of the hormone insulin by the pancreas, or a resistance to its effects around the body. It causes an increase in blood glucose levels and poisonous substances called ketones. The disease is far more common in overweight cats, and can sometimes be controlled with a strict diet. More often, cats need to go onto daily doses of insulin by injection—something many owners find less onerous and distressing than they had feared. Some diabetic cats (10–25 percent) can be managed with diet and oral hypoglycaemic medications alone.

- Because all three of these conditions can be treated or even cured if diagnosed early enough, it is important that an increase in thirst not be ignored and that a blood test be taken.

specific ailments

What you need to know about the specific problems that you and your cat might encounter.

CAN CATS GET SUNBURN?

- The cat's coat generally affords protection against the effects of exposure to excessive ultraviolet radiation from the sun, but sunburn can be a problem on the relatively bald ear tips and nose of white cats.
- This can not only be uncomfortable for the cat, but, in the long term, can also stimulate skin cancer to develop at one of these sites.
- The ultimate prevention is to keep cats indoors in summer when the sun is particularly strong, but most cats love basking in the sun and may make their owners' lives hell if prevented from doing so.
- Alternatively, you can apply a sunscreen to the exposed parts. Use a product that is known to be nontoxic to cats, such as one based on titanium dioxide.
- Because of the cat's natural inclination to clean off anything that is applied to the skin, you will have to reapply it frequently throughout the day to maintain its effect.

Even though cats enjoy sunbathing (above), too much exposure can lead to skin cancer, especially on the ear tips of white cats (right).

IS IT POSSIBLE FOR A CAT TO SUFFER FROM HEAT EXHAUSTION?

- Cats are heat-loving creatures, but they can still suffer from heat exhaustion if exposed to sufficiently high environmental temperatures for long enough.
- The most common cause of heat exhaustion is leaving cats in a car in warm weather, where the temperature can rise rapidly to 55°C (130°F), but it is also not uncommon for a cat to curl up for a snooze inside a tumble dryer, which is then switched on without anyone realising that the cat is inside.
- A cat that is suffering from excessive heat will show obvious signs of restlessness and discomfort. It will pant excessively, salivate profusely, and eventually collapse into a coma.
- The immediate treatment is to lower the body temperature by bathing the cat in cool water, but any cat that has been affected should then receive prompt veterinary attention.

WHAT ARE THE COMMON CAUSES OF POISONING IN THE CAT?

● Cats are generally fastidious about what they will eat, but because they are less able than some other animals to detoxify many poisons, they are more susceptible to their effects. The most common poisons affecting cats are the following:

● **Pharmaceuticals**

It's a sad fact that a large number of cats are accidentally poisoned by owners who administer medicine that has not been prescribed by a vet for their cat. Many drugs that are relatively safe in other species are much more toxic to cats. These include aspirin; paracetamol; and ibuprofen—three painkillers in common use.

● **Pesticides**

Again, some cases of pesticide poisoning are due to the incorrect administration of products by cat owners, the use of products that are not licensed for use in cats, or even the use in kittens of products that are licensed only for adult cats. Cats may also gain access to rodent bait, sometimes directly, but often indirectly by catching and eating a rodent that has ingested a dose of the poison. Slug bait seems to be quite palatable to cats, and quite commonly causes poisoning.

● **Skin contaminants**

These can be ingested by cats while grooming. For example, a cat could walk over spilled antifreeze in the garage and swallow some when it grooms itself. This product is lethal to pets.

● **Plants**

Many indoor and outdoor plants are potentially harmful to cats if ingested; these include ivy, poinsettia, mistletoe, laurel, foxglove, laburnum and yew. Obtain a list of poisonous plants from your vet or local garden club.

● The signs of poisoning will depend upon the substance ingested. For example, many of the rodent poisons contain anticoagulants, such as warfarin, which prevent the blood from clotting normally and cause severe internal bleeding. Many poisons cause vomiting and diarrhoea due to their irritant effect on the bowel, and affect the central nervous system producing behavioural changes, convulsions and even coma.

● **If you suspect poisoning:**

● Contact your vet without delay.

● Follow his or her instructions about giving your cat water or inducing vomiting.

● Wash any skin contaminants off and prevent any further licking.

● Take your cat to the vet along with any packaging or a sample of the poison.

- Cats have a strong tendency to worry at anything attached to their body that they think shouldn't be there, and this can include surgical stitches. Fortunately, in most cases they do not succeed, and the vast majority of wounds are left intact.

- If a cat does manage to remove some stitches, or if your vet feels unable to take that chance in a certain case, your cat may be fitted with an Elizabethan collar. This is a thin plastic cone (so named because of its slight resemblance to 16th-century starched collars) that goes over the head and attaches to the cat's identification collar, preventing the cat from getting to the wound.

WHAT IF MY CAT PULLS HER STITCHES OUT AFTER SURGERY?

DO CATS HAVE HEART ATTACKS?

- Cats do not get coronary thrombosis (blockage of the coronary arteries of the heart with fatty deposits) in the same way as humans do.

- The most common form of heart disease in cats is called cardiomyopathy and is due to a gradual failure of the heart muscle itself.

- It is also possible for cats to get cardiac arrhythmia, in which the electrical impulses that control the heart are disturbed and it fails to beat normally. This can cause sudden death due to heart failure, so in some ways could be described as a 'heart attack'.

MY CATS KEEP GETTING MILIARY DERMATITIS. WHY DOES IT RECUR?

- Miliary dermatitis is a name given to a skin condition in which the cat suffers from multiple small, itchy, scabby lesions over its body, particularly along its back.

- The most common cause is an allergic reaction, and by far the most common triggering factor is an allergy to flea bites. The cat does not have to be crawling with fleas to react in this way; the bite of a single flea, which injects its saliva into the cat, will suffice and the reaction to that one bite can last for several weeks.

- Rigorous flea control (see page 93) and a veterinary supplement of evening primrose oil may control the problem. If this does not do the trick, your vet may need to carry out further tests to try to establish the underlying cause.

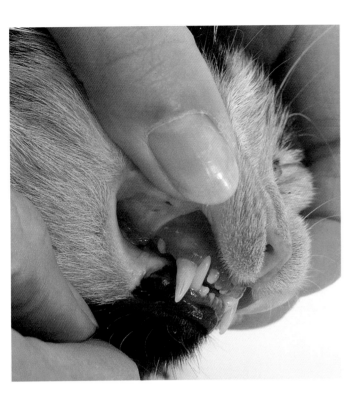

MY CAT HAS SORE GUMS AND HAS HAD ANTIBIOTICS FROM A VET. WHY ARE THEY NO BETTER?

- Chronic gingivitis, or inflammation of the gums, is a troubling condition in cats which does not respond well to treatment.
- It can be caused by an accumulation of tartar and harder, mineral-based calculus on the teeth which pushes on the gums, encouraging infection to gain a hold.
- Not all cases respond to dental de-scaling to remove the deposits, and these cats should be checked for feline leukaemia and feline immunodeficiency viruses, as both of these, and especially the latter, have been shown to play an important part in causing the problem.
- Some cats continue to have problems despite treatment for dental disease or underlying viral infections, and the only course possible is to keep them on long-term anti-inflammatory or antibiotic treatment as a means of control.

WHY IS MY CAT ANAEMIC?

- Anaemia is a shortage of circulating red blood cells, causing paleness of the mucous membranes in the mouth and around the eyes, combined with weakness and breathlessness due to a lack of oxygen to the body.
- It can be caused by a failure to produce enough blood cells, by the excessive breakdown of these cells, or by a loss of red blood cells due to chronic bleeding, either externally or internally into a body cavity.
- Many different conditions can, in turn, cause these distinct types of anaemia; examples of each, respectively, are bone marrow disease due to lymphosarcoma (a kind of tumour), infectious anaemia due to parasitism of the red blood cells with a parasite called *Hemobartonella felis*, and internal bleeding due to injury or blood-clotting problems. A common cause is fleas.
- A blood test, as well as a thorough clinical examination, will help to identify and, ideally, treat the cause.

MY ELDERLY CAT HAS LOST HER BALANCE. IS THIS LIKELY TO BE DUE TO A STROKE?

- Although cats do not get blockage of the arteries with fatty deposits, as humans do, they do suffer from a condition in which the blood supply to one part of the brain is suddenly lost.
- Other possible causes of a loss of balance—or ataxia—are brain tumours and inner ear infections. These conditions may cross the eardrum or travel up the Eustachian tube, which connects the back of the throat to the middle ear, and then damage the organs of balance deep in the inner ear.

- Conjunctivitis is an inflammation of the membrane, called the conjunctiva, that lines the surface of the eye and the inner lining of the eyelids. It is a common condition in cats, and has many different causes.

WHAT ARE THE MAIN CAUSES OF CONJUNCTIVITIS IN A CAT?

- Minor injuries and physical irritation of the eye with substances such as pollen or dust can inflame the conjunctiva. This can then lead to a secondary infection involving bacteria normally present in harmless numbers in the conjunctival sac, which take advantage of the weakened defence mechanisms to multiply out of control.
- Infections can be passed from cat to cat, and conjunctivitis is frequently seen as part of a more generalised problem such as cat flu.
- Deformities of the lids or ingrown eyelashes can irritate the surface of the eye and cause conjunctivitis, and in longhair cats with flattened faces, the hairs of the nose can rub onto the eye.

MY CAT KEEPS GETTING CYSTITIS, DESPITE BEING FED A SPECIAL DIET. WHAT MORE CAN I DO?

- Cats most commonly get bladder problems because they produce crystals in the urine that irritate the lining of the bladder, and in male cats these can even obstruct the flow of urine entirely.
- Diet plays a major role in the production of these crystals, and special diets that are low in magnesium and produce an acidic urine have been used effectively for some time to dissolve these crystals. There is now an increasing incidence of a different type of crystal, which is not as easy to prevent, and requires a different type of diet.
- Your vet may want to X-ray your cat's bladder to ensure that there are no other problems, such as large stones or a growth within the bladder. A sample of urine can also then be analysed to check for any infection and to see what type of crystals are present, so that your cat can go onto the correct diet.
- Sometimes the recurrent cystitis can be stress related, and some cats do well with a mild dose of a sedative.

CAN CATS HAVE CATARACT OPERATIONS?

- Yes. Provided that the retina, at the back of the eye, is functioning normally, it is possible to remove a lens that has become cloudy and restore vision.
- However, primary cataracts, without any other concurrent eye disease, are fortunately quite rare in cats.

- Jaundice is an accumulation of bile pigments in the body seen as a yellowing of the skin, the mucous membranes (such as the gums) and the whites of the eyes.
- Bile pigments are found in large quantities in the red blood cells, and when these cells become aged and are broken down in the body, the pigments are excreted via the liver, down the gall duct, and into the faeces. A buildup of bile pigments can occur if excessive amounts of red blood cells are being destroyed, if the liver is diseased and unable to cope with processing the bile, or if there is an obstruction to the flow of bile out of the liver, such as by a tumour blocking the bile duct. Blood tests are needed to identify the underlying cause of the jaundice so that it can be treated.

WHAT IS JAUNDICE, AND HOW CAN IT BE TREATED?

WHAT IS CAT SCRATCH FEVER?

- This is of no significance as a disease of cats, for cats can carry the bacterium, called *Bartonella*, that causes the problem without showing any ill effects at all.
- It is, rather, humans who suffer from this infection, having contracted it from cat scratches or bites. The disease is usually mild, with some swelling around the wound, followed by enlargement of nearby lymph glands.
- If the person's immune system is compromised by disease problems such as human immunodeficiency virus (HIV) infection or by the administration of immunosuppressive drugs, the organism can spread to other parts of the body such as the brain and the bone marrow and cause severe illness. Fortunately, this is fairly rare.
- It is advisable to obtain medical advice if any signs of illness develop after you are bitten or scratched by a cat.

HOW DO CATS GET DIAPHRAGMATIC HERNIAS?

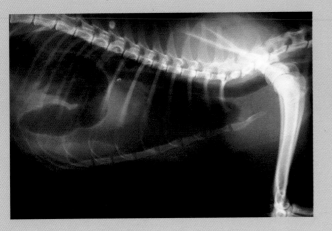

- The diaphragm is a sheet of muscle and fibrous tissue that separates the chest cavity from the abdomen and plays an important part in assisting breathing.
- If a cat receives a major blow to the chest when its larynx is closed, the sudden increase of pressure within the chest can cause the diaphragm to tear.
- This is quite common after a road accident or a fall from a height, and in some cases the owner may not be aware it has happened. The breathing will be more rapid than usual, but if the condition is left untreated, the cat will sometimes adapt to the injury and seem fairly normal.
- Abdominal parts, such as the stomach or a lobe of the liver, may then pass up into the chest and suddenly cause severe respiratory distress and even death.
- This is one reason why a cat should always be checked after an accident, and have its chest X-rayed if there is any doubt.

parasites

How to recognise and deal with parasitic infestation in your cat.

HOW DO I KNOW IF MY CAT HAS WORMS?

- Adult roundworms live in the intestine and shed microscopically small eggs into the faeces, so you may become aware of a problem only if your cat happens to vomit up a worm or pass it in its faeces.
- You are more likely to notice tapeworms—which appear as white, ricelike segments around your cat's anal area or in its stools.
- Lungworm can be detected only by laboratory analysis of faecal samples to search for the larvae that they shed.
- I recommend that any cats that are considered to be at risk should be wormed regularly, whether or not actual signs of worms are seen.

HOW OFTEN SHOULD I WORM MY CAT?

- This will depend on the lifestyle of your cat. No worming medication will entirely prevent your cat from getting worms, so you have to repeat it often enough to deal with any re-infestation that may occur.
- The three main types of worms that cats may get are roundworms, which are long and stringlike, live in the intestines, and are picked up either by a kitten from its mother or by hunting and eating wildlife; lungworms which are smaller and live within the airways, causing a mild cough that is usually self-limiting (these, too, are contracted during hunting); and tapeworms which are long and flat (the adult lives firmly attached to the intestine wall and sheds segments called proglottids into the faeces; although these may be contracted from wildlife, they can also be picked up from fleas).
- If your cat is an indoor cat and free of fleas, it will need worming only infrequently, if at all. However, if your cat is an active hunter, then it should be wormed about every three months—more often if any signs of worms or fleas are seen.
- Coccidiosis is a common parasitism of cats and can cause diarrhoea, occasional vomiting, weight loss, and dehydration, especially in kittens. One type of coccidiosis is toxoplasmosis which can infect humans.
- Heartworm can also occur in cats. Transmitted by blood-sucking insects, it is less common in cats than dogs but can sometimes cause serious heart and breathing problems. You should contact your vet for further specific advice if you live in an area where this disease occurs.

IS WORMING MEDICATION SAFE FOR MY CAT?

- Modern worming medication, unlike some of the more old-fashioned products, is now very safe and effective, and can clear tapeworms and roundworms with just a single dose.
- Your vet is the best person to turn to for advice about worming your cat.

WHERE DO MY CATS PICK UP FLEAS?

- Cat fleas need a warm environment to breed, and will breed out of doors only in semitropical areas. Therefore, your cat will pick up most of the fleas that infest it from inside your home.
- The eggs are laid by the fleas on the cat, but drop off onto the floor, where they hatch into larvae. These tiny maggotlike creatures wriggle into the darkest recesses of the house, where they feed on shed skin cells from their host and the droppings of adult fleas. They then form very resistant pupae, and wait in their cocoons patiently for their victim to pass. They will wait for several months, then hatch out in seconds in response to vibrations and to carbon dioxide exhaled by humans or pets, jumping large distances to hitch a ride.
- It is therefore essential that any treatment to eradicate fleas includes thorough fumigation of the environment. Ask your vet about effective products for this purpose.

WHY ARE FLEAS SO COMMON?

- Cat fleas are far more common nowadays than dog fleas.
- There's nothing a flea loves more than a heated and fully carpeted environment.
- The warm, humid, sometimes poorly ventilated homes that so many of us live in have resulted in a massive increase in the flea population.

HOW CAN I STOP MY CAT FROM GETTING FLEAS?

- Cat owners are strongly advised to carry out regular preventive treatment before their homes become infested, instead of waiting for a problem to become evident before taking action.
- Several new, safe and very effective veterinary products for eliminating fleas are now available. Some have a residual insecticidal action to kill fleas over an extended period; others interfere with the life cycle of the flea and prevent them from breeding. They are also easy to apply, being available in drop-on formulations or as liquids designed to be given by mouth.
- These are far more effective than collars and powders—particularly the organophosphorus-based products, which have now been replaced by safer, more reliable drugs.

Flea eggs laid around the home.

WILL FLEAS BITE HUMANS?

- They certainly will, although they will not live out their normal life cycle without a cat or dog being present.
- Some humans are more susceptible to being bitten than others, but we don't know why this is so.

- No. Although cats, and especially kittens, can get lice, these lice are very fussy about which species they inhabit and will not infest humans.

MY CHILDREN HAVE HEAD LICE. COULD THEY HAVE GOT THEM FROM MY CAT?

- You may spot the adult lice moving on your cat's fur, but more often you may spot the louse eggs, or nits, stuck to the hairs.
- Because they live their whole life cycle on the cat, they can easily be eradicated with veterinary insecticides, although treatment must be continued until all the eggs have hatched.

- Ear mites are tiny eight-legged animals that live down in the ear canal and feed on ear wax.
- The irritation that they cause stimulates the ear to produce a lot more dark wax, and usually results in the cat doing a lot of ear scratching and head shaking.
- Drops can be put into the ear to kill off the

HOW CAN I GET RID OF EAR MITES?

mites and soften the wax, but any course of treatment must be continued for at least three weeks to kill off any eggs that may be present, and all dogs and cats in the household must be treated to prevent cross-infection.

- The thing not to do is just to pull it off, as there is a strong chance that you will leave the head buried in the skin, which can set up a nasty reaction.
- Ticks are wingless, blood-sucking arachnids which are picked up from long grass; they fill their body with blood in one enormous meal, then drop off the host animal.

WHAT SHOULD I DO IF MY CAT PICKS UP A TICK?

- To kill the tick, apply an insecticidal spray directly onto it. Once the tick has died, it will shrivel up and lose its grip. It will then probably drop off by itself; if not, you can then pull it off easily.
- If the area around the bite becomes inflamed or your cat becomes ill, seek veterinary attention.

Severe ear inflammation caused by mites.

CAN RINGWORM BE TRANSMITTED TO HUMANS?

- Yes. Ringworm is a fungus that grows on the hair, and is quite common in kittens.
- It causes bald, scaly patches, especially around the head. If you suspect ringworm, you should wash your hands thoroughly after handling your pet and seek veterinary attention without delay.
- Ringworm can usually be treated successfully, but because the drugs to treat the problem have to grow into the hair to be effective, treatment must be repeated for several weeks.
- Clipping short the coat of longhaired cats and applying topical washes will help, and all grooming implements must be treated to avoid re-contamination.

Ringworm lesions over the eye of a white kitten.

infections & diseases

Causes and symptoms of infection, diseases that your cat can catch, and how to prevent and treat them.

WHAT CAUSES CAT FLU?

- The most common causes of cat flu are two viruses, feline calicivirus and feline viral rhinotracheitis virus, that cause different disease patterns.
- These two vaccines are given annually, but there are other bugs that can also cause flu-like signs and that are not normally included in the vaccinations.
- This is the main reason why vaccinations in cats are not 100 percent effective. Vaccinated cats that do contract cat flu generally seem to get it more mildly.

Severe conjunctivitis is a typical symptom of cat flu.

WHAT DISEASE PROBLEMS ARE CAUSED BY FELINE LEUKAEMIA VIRUS?

- It can affect the immune system of the cat, causing an AIDS-like syndrome, which lowers the cat's defence against infection.
- It can also cause severe anaemia (a deficiency of red blood cells), infertility, or cancers of the white blood cells, often a considerable time after the original infection. This results in leukaemia, a cancer of the white blood cells circulating in the blood stream, or lymphosarcoma, a cancer of the white blood cells that are present in the lymphatic tissue around the body.
- The clinical signs that develop will depend upon where within the body these growths develop, but the lymph nodes within the chest in young cats or in the intestines of older cats are common sites.
- Fortunately, we now have a vaccine to help protect against this very serious feline virus.

DO CATS EVER COMPLETELY RECOVER FROM VIRUS INFECTIONS?

- Cats that are infected with feline calicivirus may get over the illness but remain carriers for several months.
- The situation with feline viral rhinotracheitis virus is worse, as the virus lurks in the body for years after the initial bout of illness, often without causing any visible symptoms.
- Then, if the cat is stressed, the latent virus is able to take advantage of the cat's immune system, and the cat may become infectious again and show clinical signs, such as sneezing and runny eyes.

- Feline infectious peritonitis (FIP) is quite a common condition of cats which is caused by feline coronavirus. This virus is often found in cats but does not usually cause any significant illness.
- The virus constantly mutates into new forms, and disease develops only if it changes into a form that is harmful. It then upsets the immune system of the cat and results in one of two forms of the disease: wet FIP, in which fluid accumulates in the abdomen or within the chest; or, less commonly, dry FIP, in which multiple nodules can develop in many sites around the body, but quite often in the eye or in the brain. Once a cat develops this condition, it is invariably fatal.
- The disease is much more common in multi-cat households, especially where a lot of cats are sharing the same litter tray and cross-infecting each other with their different strains of the virus; but it is not uncommon for just one cat to fall ill and the others to be unaffected.
- The blood test is of little value in diagnosis, because it cannot tell the difference between the different strains of the virus. A cat that has a high positive result may stay perfectly healthy, and one with a negative result may be dying with FIP.
- All you can do is to provide at least one litter tray for every two cats and clean them out regularly.

ONE OF MY CATS HAD A POSITIVE BLOOD TEST FOR FELINE INFECTIOUS PERITONITIS AND IS VERY ILL. WILL MY OTHER CATS CATCH IT?

- A relatively new vaccine against feline coronavirus is now available in some countries, but its use is not without problems. First, it is less than 80 percent effective at preventing the disease; second, if given to cats that already have antibodies to the virus in their blood, it may accelerate the course of the illness. It also has to be given in drop form into the nose after 16 weeks of age, which can be quite difficult with some cats.
- Many cats that test positive for feline coronavirus never develop FIP. Others, of course, do; but unfortunately the vaccine should be used only in cats that have been tested and found to be negative.
- This limits the usefulness of vaccination as a means of controlling FIP at the present time, but if you are particularly concerned, you could have your cat blood-tested and vaccinated if it is antibody-negative (and if the vaccine is available in your area).

SHOULD I HAVE MY CAT VACCINATED AGAINST FELINE INFECTIOUS PERITONITIS?

- No. AIDS is not a single disease, but a combination of signs, which can be caused by more than one agent, that attack the immune system and make the cat more prone to other illnesses. Feline leukaemia virus can cause suppression of the immune system, but the cat can also be infected with feline immunodeficiency virus.
- Fortunately, current evidence shows that neither of these viruses is transmitted from cats to humans.
- We do not yet have a vaccine against feline immunodeficiency virus.

CAN WE GET AIDS FROM CATS?

- Inflammatory bowel disease (IBD) is the most common cause of chronic vomiting and diarrhoea in cats.
- The cause is not fully understood, but it is a group of conditions that result in an irritability of the lining of the intestines.
- In some cases, the triggering factor is found to be a particular substance in the diet, and treatment can consist solely of feeding a non-irritant diet, but very often long-term anti-inflammatory treatment with a drug such as prednisolone is necessary to keep it under control.

WHAT IS INFLAMMATORY BOWEL DISEASE?

IS THERE ANY CURE FOR CATS WITH CANCER?

- The answer is a qualified yes. Cancer is not just one disease, but many—all caused by an uncontrolled proliferation of a certain type of cell. Some cancers are fairly benign and will not grow back or spread if they are surgically removed, whereas others are highly malignant and will invade the surrounding tissues and spread to other parts of the body, causing death in a fairly short time regardless of the treatment given. In between these two extremes are many types of cancer that can be controlled with a combination of treatments to give a cat a useful extra lease on life.
- Besides surgery to remove any isolated masses, chemotherapy (treatment with drugs) is often used, particularly with lymphosarcoma, in which very good results can be achieved. Radiotherapy is also now becoming available as an option for cats in some of the more advanced treatment centres, often as a follow-up to surgery to prevent a tumour from growing back.

ARE CATS LIKELY TO PASS ON RABIES TO HUMANS?

- Rabies is a horrific disease which attacks the central nervous system of any warm-blooded animal it infects, leading to severe behavioural changes, convulsions and death. The virus is found in the saliva of infected animals and is spread mainly by biting, although it can also enter the body through a contaminated scratch or wound.
- In Europe and Canada the main reservoirs of the disease are red foxes, whereas in the United States it is the raccoon and the skunk that are mainly responsible for carrying the disease. Some countries, such as the United Kingdom, Australia and New Zealand, have been able to remain free of the disease by maintaining strict controls on the movement of animals.

- Dogs are fairly susceptible to the virus, and in some countries, such as India, the domestic dog is a major reservoir of infection, posing a particularly strong health risk to humans.
- Cats are also fairly commonly infected with rabies in areas where it is endemic in the wildlife, but research shows that they seem less likely than dogs to pass it on to other animals.
- Very effective vaccines against rabies in cats now exist, and it is recommended (and in some places compulsory) that cats be vaccinated in areas where rabies is found.
- Any human who even suspects that he or she may have come into contact with a rabid animal should disinfect any bites or wounds thoroughly and contact a doctor without delay.

how to treat

The best ways to administer medication to your sick cat.

- Great care must be taken when force-feeding a cat to ensure that you do not do more harm than good.
- Unless your cat agrees to eat with some coaxing, you are very unlikely to be able to get significant amounts of solid food down, and you are going to need to use a liquid food.
- Several commercial brands of liquid cat food are now available through veterinary clinics, and they are thin enough to be squirted through a syringe.
- You will need one person to hold the cat, wrapping its legs in a towel, to prevent it from scratching, and the other person to bend the head back over the neck until the lower jaw drops open.
- The food can then be dribbled into the mouth, but it is important that this be done very slowly so that the cat does not inhale the liquid rather than swallow it.

HOW CAN YOU NOURISH A SICK CAT THAT REFUSES TO TAKE FOOD OR WATER?

- If a cat steadfastly refuses to eat or drink for more than a couple of days, and cannot readily be force-fed, as described left, your vet will need to take steps to provide the cat with an alternative source of nourishment.
- Fluids and minerals are the most important in the short term, and these can be given by a subcutaneous route or by an intravenous drip.
- Supplying food intravenously is much more difficult, and if a cat is unable or unwilling to eat for an extended period, your vet may decide to place a feeding tube in the cat under a topical anaesthetic.
- The most common form is a nasogastric tube, which is very fine and passes down the nose and into the stomach. This is tolerated by cats surprisingly well and can be left in place for several weeks if necessary.

HOW CAN I FORCE-FEED MY SICK CAT?

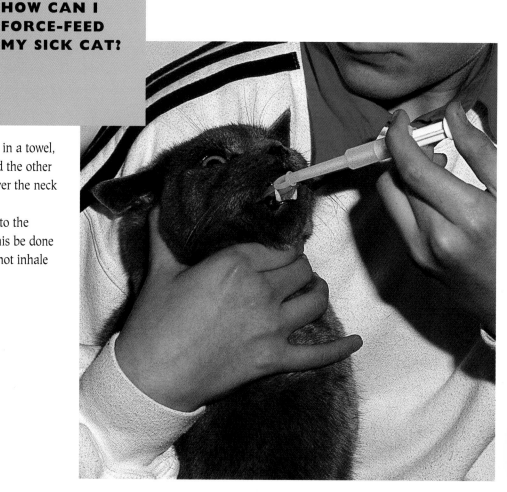

HOW ON EARTH CAN I COLLECT A URINE SAMPLE FOR TESTING FROM MY CAT?

- This is a procedure that you may be asked to do by your vet—possibly on a regular basis. If your cat is diabetic or suffers from recurrent urinary problems, its urine may require regular testing.
- The first step is to get your cat accustomed to using a litter tray if it does not already do so.
- Then you will need to obtain some special nonabsorbent cat litter made for this purpose; or you can use some thoroughly washed aquarium gravel. Put a layer of this into the tray. The urine will not be absorbed and can be collected from the tray after the cat has performed.
- You need to keep the sample cool and have it checked by your vet as soon as possible.
- If you put the sample into a jar, make sure that any traces of food have been washed out thoroughly, or a false reading for sugar in the urine could result.

IF MY CAT HAS A MINOR INJURY, WHAT DISINFECTANT CAN I USE?

- Take great care with your choice, because although you are using it topically, it will be licked off and ingested by your cat.
- Many disinfectants are based on chemicals that may be toxic to cats.
- I would advise that any wounds be simply bathed in a solution of one teaspoon of salt to 500 ml (1 pint) of warm water. This will not sting at this concentration, and will help to keep the wound clean.
- If the wound starts to discharge or becomes hot and tender, or if the cat is ill, antibiotics may be needed.

HOW DO I GIVE A PILL TO MY CAT?

- And why am I so proficient at giving tablets to other people's cats and so inept at giving them to my own?
- If the tablet cannot be given in food, or the cat refuses to take it, the procedure is almost the same as force-feeding a cat with liquids (see opposite). This, too, is best accomplished with a helper and with the cat wrapped in a towel.
- Instead of dribbling liquid into the mouth, you have to open the mouth further with one finger, and use a finger and thumb of the other hand to hold the tablet and push it right to the back of the cat's throat, so that it has to be swallowed.
- Greasing the tablet with a little butter will help it slip down more easily.
- Pill holders, which grasp the pill and then release it with a plunger mechanism may save your fingers.

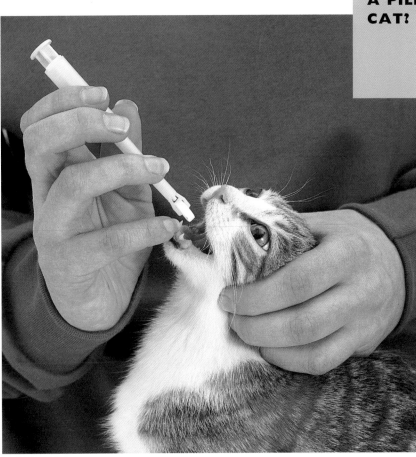

- This is another two-person task, with one person holding the cat and the other administering the drops.
- The trick is to hold onto the ear flap really firmly, so that the cat cannot shake its head, until you have had a chance to drop the medicine into the ear and then to massage the liquid well down into the ear.
- You can then let go and start cleaning the spots off the wallpaper.

HOW CAN I PUT DROPS INTO MY CAT'S EARS?

- With your trusty assistant steadying the cat, you need to use one hand to hold the head and pull down the lower eyelid.
- Hold the dropper bottle or tube in the other hand, squeeze it to allow some of the medication to fall into the conjunctival sac that is found between the lower eyelid and the eye.
- Avoid touching the open end of the container against the cat's eye—or anything else.
- Never use an eye ointment or drops that have been open for more than six weeks. Always double check that the ointment is specifically labelled for use in the eye.

HOW CAN I PUT OINTMENT INTO MY CAT'S EYES?

alternative medicine

What you need to know about alternative ways of treating your cat.

- There is much confusion between herbalism and homoeopathy in the mind of the public.
- Homoeopathic remedies work on the principle of 'like curing like', and contain minuscule amounts of substances that in larger doses would cause the signs of illness that are troubling the patient.

ARE HERBAL AND HOMOEO-PATHIC REMEDIES SAFE TO USE ON CATS?

- There is no scientific evidence for its effectiveness, so its use is largely a matter of faith, but there is no likelihood that a homoeopathic remedy could do harm.
- Herbal extracts have been used for thousands of years to treat illness in humans and animals, and many of our efficacious modern drugs are derived from plant-based products.

- Keep your tea for drinking and take your cat to the vet for an examination and the proper treatment.
- Problems such as corneal ulcers may get worse if left untreated, and can even result in a loss of vision.

MY CAT HAS A VERY SORE EYE, AND I HAVE HEARD YOU CAN BATHE IT IN WEAK TEA. WILL THIS HELP?

- Herbalists believe that many drugs work more gently and more effectively if given in their naturally occurring form, rather than as purified pharmaceutical products. This may sometimes be the case, but it should not be assumed that herbal products are always harmless. They contain potent compounds, and the cat may sometimes be more susceptible than other species to their poisonous effects.
- Never give herbal medicine unless you are certain it is safe for your cat.

There are many hazards facing a young and inexperienced cat, especially Feline Public Enemy Number One—the automobile. Even cats that live indoors, protected from its lethal wheels, may take flying leaps off high balconies, or chew electric wires and electrocute themselves. A cat that survives its first couple of years of life may live well into its teenage years; but the average age for the domestic cat is less than that because of young cats that die early.

A basic knowledge of first aid—as it applies to cats—can be life-saving in an emergency situation, but it is no substitute for veterinary care. With a serious injury, the priority is to take the cat to a vet after first aid has been carried out.

Make sure that you are familiar with the

7 First aid

emergency procedure at your veterinary clinic. Some offer a 24-hour service on the premises, some may have a rotation system with neighbouring practices, and others make use of a central emergency hospital that covers a wide area. This may mean travelling a greater distance, but it means that trained staff and equipment are available around the clock to deal with injuries. Find out about the emergency service that your practice offers by calling the normal number, which should have a 24-hour answering service. Resist the temptation to pick up your injured cat and go to the nearest veterinary facility. You may find a vet, but you may just be referred to the duty clinician. Telephone ahead to make arrangements, even in the daytime.

cat crises

How to care for your cat in an emergency situation.

HOW CAN I TELL IF MY CAT NEEDS IMMEDIATE VETERINARY ATTENTION?

- Common sense should dictate when urgent veterinary care is needed, but some of the most common emergencies include:
- Any severe injury from a road accident, or a serious fall.
- A wound that is bleeding profusely or gaping open.
- Repeated and severe vomiting, with or without diarrhoea, especially if you think the cat may have swallowed something harmful.
- Choking or markedly laboured breathing.
- Severe burns and scalds.
- Heat stroke, or loss of consciousness for any reason.
- A fit that lasts for more than ten minutes.
- Straining to pass urine, particularly in a male cat.

HOW CAN I GET VETERINARY HELP IN AN EMERGENCY?

- All veterinary practices should have emergency arrangements for their clients, although this may be organised with other local practices on a rotation basis, or based at a central emergency clinic.
- You will normally be able to contact the emergency service after hours by telephoning the usual number, where your call may be automatically forwarded or passed on by an answering service.
- It is probably wise to check out what emergency arrangements your practice runs before the need arises.

WHAT SHOULD I HAVE IN MY FELINE FIRST AID KIT?

- It is well worth preparing a basic first aid kit specifically for your cat, to avoid any frantic rushes to a pharmacy if a problem occurs. The first aid kit should include:
- Bandages and gauze swabs—for applying pressure to bleeding wounds.
- Scissors—'round on flat' nursing scissors are the best.
- Syringe or plastic eyedropper—for administering liquids.
- Antiseptic skin ointment—make sure it is one that is safe for cats.
- Mineral oil (liquid paraffin) gel—as a treatment for hairballs or constipation.
- Waterless hand cleanser—for removing tar or paint from the cat's coat (do NOT use solvents such as turpentine).
- Paediatric kaolin—for diarrhoea. Use only at your vet's direction.
- Phone numbers of veterinary clinic and poison control centre.
- Also, make sure that you have a sturdy cat carrier, which is essential if you have to transport your cat to a vet in an emergency.

IS IT POSSIBLE TO REVIVE A CAT THAT HAS DROWNED?

- If you think the cat may still be alive, hold it upside down by its hind legs between your own legs, and gently swing the cat backward and forward.
- This will use gravity to drain the water out of its lungs. If it is still not breathing, you should try cardiopulmonary resuscitation (CPR), as described below.

- Yes, but only to a limited extent.

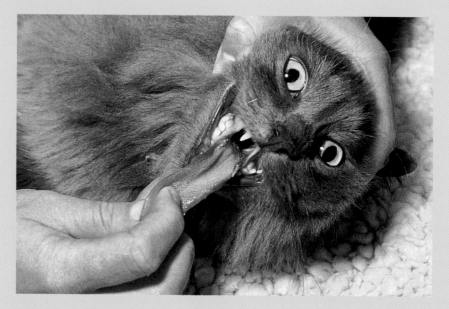

- Make sure that the cat is able to breathe easily by clearing any fluid or debris from the mouth and gently pulling the tongue forward, but while doing this, be very careful to avoid getting bitten.

IS IT POSSIBLE TO ADMINISTER CPR TO A CAT?

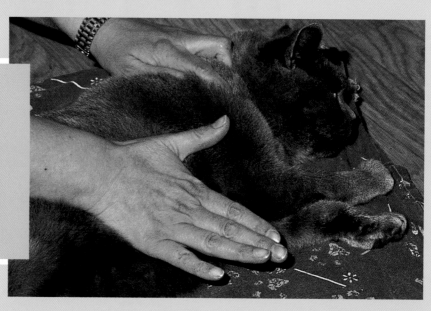

- You can attempt artificial respiration by compressing the chest with your hand once every couple of seconds to force air out of the lungs.
- Some pet first aid books recommend mouth-to-nose resuscitation for cats, but it is unlikely to be effective, and you could easily end up with a bad injury.

- Insect stings are common, especially in the summer months, because cats find flying insects just too fascinating to resist—including those covered in yellow and black stripes.
- Stings usually occur on the front feet or around the mouth, and can cause quite a lot of pain and swelling.
- Bee stings should be bathed in a solution of bicarbonate of soda (baking soda) to neutralise their acidity, whereas wasp stings are alkaline and can be neutralised by bathing in vinegar and water; if you're not sure which insect it was, leave the sting alone.
- Some cats are allergic to stings, and get a generalised reaction with swelling. In this case, the cat should receive veterinary attention without delay.
- If you know that your cat reacts in this way, you could ask your vet about keeping some antihistamine tablets on hand.

WHAT SHOULD I DO IF MY CAT IS STUNG?

WHAT CAN I DO IF MY CAT IS BITTEN BY A VENOMOUS SNAKE?

- Cats are usually bitten on the face or legs. Although many snakes are not venomous, if you see small bite wounds close together, assume that it is.
- Keep the cat as quiet as possible to slow down the absorption of the poison, and seek immediate veterinary advice. Be prepared to identify the species of snake if you can.
- If you live in an area where venomous snake bites are common, your vet should have the appropriate antiserum.

major injury

First aid for cats, and how to deal with severely injured cats.

- First, get yourself and your cat out of any further danger from moving cars.
- A cat that has been hit by a vehicle should always be examined by a veterinarian, even if it seems unharmed externally, as there may be internal injuries that need treating.
- If the cat is unconscious, make sure that its airway is clear.
- Try to stanch any serious bleeding with a pressure bandage, and contact the veterinary clinic quickly to arrange for emergency treatment.
- If the cat is unconscious, slide it onto a towel and use as a support to pick the cat up with the minimum of disturbance.
- Do not splint any broken bones, for you will almost certainly cause further damage as the cat struggles, and do not give anything by mouth, in case an anaesthetic has to be administered. There is also a danger that the cat will inhale anything given by mouth.

- Strange as it may seem, it can be difficult to distinguish between a deeply unconscious cat and one that is dead.
- The following conditions are signs that the cat's death has occurred:
- The pupils of the eyes become widely dilated and unresponsive to light. There is no blink reflex if the surface of the eye is touched.
- Breathing will have ceased. Watch the chest for movement, or hold a wisp of cotton wool in front of the nostrils. If the cotton wool does not move, the cat is dead.
- The heartbeat will have stopped. You can feel a heartbeat if you put a finger and thumb on each side of the chest, just behind the elbows, or you can see the hairs of the chest wall moving as the heart beats underneath.
- If in any doubt, obtain veterinary advice without delay.

- Shock is a collapse of the circulation. It can be due to many different causes, such as blood or fluid loss, heart failure, major allergic reactions and serious infections.
- This results in signs such as weakness, a rapid pulse, pale mucous membranes such as the gums, shallow breathing and cold extremities.
- Whatever the cause, shock can rapidly prove fatal unless treated promptly and aggressively.
- Initially this involves stemming any significant blood loss and keeping the patient comfortably warm until veterinary assistance can be obtained. Intensive treatment may be needed to reverse shock—chiefly by the administration of large amounts of intravenous fluids to restore the circulating blood volume.
- Drugs, such as large doses of corticosteroids and vasodilators to open up the blood supply to the tissues, can be of value.

Checking a shocked cat's pulse rate.

- Keep a secure cat carrier on hand in case it is required (in an emergency a sturdy cardboard box will suffice).
- If the cat struggles when someone attempts to move it, throw a large towel over it and pick it up as a bundle, placing the cat and the towel in the carrier together.
- A frightened cat will run off if it can, and may bite and scratch in its efforts to escape, so handle it very cautiously, wearing thick leather gloves if you have them available.

WHAT IS THE BEST WAY TO MOVE AN INJURED CAT?

- No. First, you should not give anything by mouth, as the cat may need to have an anaesthetic. Second, many painkillers that are safe in other species are very toxic to cats. This includes drugs such as aspirin, paracetamol and ibuprofen.
- Give only painkillers that are specifically prescribed by your vet for your cat.

SHOULD I GIVE AN INJURED CAT A PAINKILLING TABLET?

- Try to stop serious bleeding by applying firm pressure with a pad of gauze and a bandage over the wound.
- However, avoid struggling with the cat, as you will only raise its blood pressure and make the bleeding worse.
- Take the cat immediately to a veterinary clinic, so that steps can be taken to stop any bleeding; replacement fluid therapy can be given intravenously if blood loss is severe. A blood transfusion may be indicated as well.

WHAT IF MY CAT IS BLEEDING BADLY FROM A WOUND?

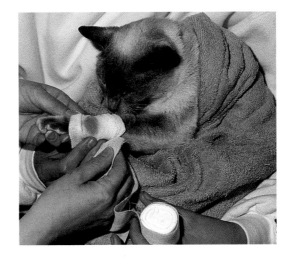

SHOULD BROKEN BONES BE SPLINTED?

- No. If a cat has a fracture of any significance, it is going to be far too painful for you to be able to do anything constructive in the way of a splint, and there is a strong chance that you will do more harm than good.
- A struggling cat will cause more bruising and bleeding at the site of the fracture, and the broken bone may even pierce the skin, allowing infection to enter.
- The cat will need to be anaesthetised or heavily sedated so that it can be X-rayed and treated appropriately by a vet. Many feline fractures are treated by internal fixation, in which a metal pin or plate is implanted surgically, as cats do not tolerate splints or plaster casts very well.

To keep a shocked cat warm and quiet, wrap it in a towel or blanket.

other worries

How to assess whether your cat is in need of professional attention.

MY CAT KEEPS GETTING INTO FIGHTS AND DEVELOPING ABSCESSES. HOW SHOULD THEY BE TREATED?

- Abscesses resulting from a cat bite are probably the most common reason for a cat to be being taken to a vet.
- If you think your cat has been bitten, you should clean the wound thoroughly with an antiseptic that is safe for cats, and watch it carefully for any signs of infection, such as tenderness, swelling, discharge, an abnormal smell or changes in behaviour.
- At the first of any of these signs you should take your cat to the vet, as antibiotics are very often needed to treat severe bites.
- Once infection gains a hold, the bite may quickly swell into an abscess, full of pus. This needs to be brought to a head so that it bursts open or can be lanced by a vet.
- Bathing the affected area three times a day in a solution of one teaspoonful of salt to 500 ml (1 pint) of water, as warm as the cat will comfortably tolerate, will help greatly.
- Once the abscess bursts, the bathing should be continued, and the hole kept open for as long as possible to allow all the infection to drain out.
- Antibiotic treatment should be continued until all the infection has completely cleared.

MY CAT KEEPS CHEWING ON ELECTRIC CABLES. IS HE LIKELY TO GET ELECTROCUTED?

- Yes. This pastime is most definitely not recommended. Obviously, you can try to prevent problems by making sure that all electrical cords are pulled out of the sockets if the cat is left unattended.
- This behaviour justifies drastic action, and you should find out about some type of aversion therapy to stop it.
- If your cat should get electrocuted, it will almost certainly suffer serious burns to its mouth, if it survives at all.
- Make sure the electrical supply is switched off before touching your cat, and arrange emergency veterinary care.

- Panicking is never a good idea, but there is a big difference in urgency between constipation and an inability to urinate.
- The latter condition should be watched out for, especially in male cats, who are far more likely than females to get an obstruction due to the narrowness of their urethra, the tube that carries the urine from the bladder out of the body.

SHOULD I PANIC IF MY CAT IS STRAINING TO URINATE OR DEFECATE?

- It is therefore essential to establish what is causing the straining, and if you suspect a urinary blockage, seek immediate veterinary attention; otherwise, irreversible damage to the bladder could result.

HOW CAN I HELP MY CAT IF HE SEEMS TO BE CHOKING?

- Cats occasionally get objects trapped in the mouth, such as a piece of chicken bone or a needle and thread. This will cause considerable discomfort, drooling and pawing at the mouth, but will not interfere with the cat's breathing.
- Although this requires urgent attention, an even more serious problem exists if there is something obstructing the passage of air into the cat's chest. The cat will become very distressed, the tongue and mucous membranes of the mouth will acquire a marked bluish tint and collapse and death may rapidly follow.
- Reaching into the throat of a panicking cat to try to clear an obstruction is dangerous and unlikely to be successful; it can be done relatively easily if the cat is unconscious.
- In a conscious cat, you could try sharply compressing the chest between your hands in the hope that the rapid exhalation of air forces the offending item out of the throat.
- The cat should still receive a veterinary examination to make sure that secondary problems are not due to swelling in the throat.

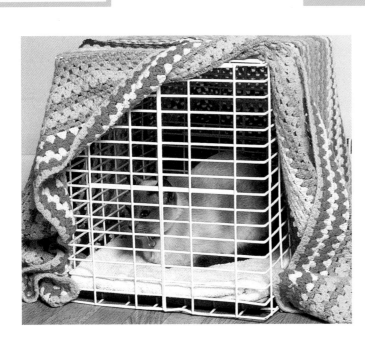

WHAT SHOULD I DO IF MY CAT HAS A FIT?

- It is best not to disturb a cat while it is having a fit—just make sure it is out of harm's way, preferably in a dark, quiet room, and keep it under observation.
- If the fit lasts for more than ten minutes, or if the cat has more than one fit in quick succession, urgent veterinary attention is required.
- Otherwise, the cat should be checked over once the convulsions have ceased, to try to establish what the underlying cause has been. Long-term anti-convulsant treatment may be necessary in some severe cases.

8 Breeding & Neutering

I make no apologies for the strong emphasis on having your cat neutered. Animal shelters are overflowing with cats and kittens looking for good homes. However, the fact that you're reading this book shows that you are a responsible cat owner, and so information has been included that will be useful if you have decided to breed your cat, trusting that you have carefully thought about finding good homes for all the kittens.

The sexual behaviour of the domestic cat is enough to make even the most liberal-minded gasp. A queen in season calls far and wide for any willing male to mate with her and a queen may carry kittens with more than one father.

The mating process is short and, literally, sharp. The female cat releases the eggs to be fertilised only as a response to mating. The male grasps the female by the scruff of her neck with his teeth, which holds her in place while he penetrates her. His penis has sharp spines that cause pain when he withdraws, stimulating the queen to ovulate. A queen's mating season usually starts in late winter, and may last into the summer. This ceases only if she is mated, when the calling ceases and all is quiet until the kittens arrive.

basic instincts

Factors to consider before you start breeding your cat.

AT WHAT AGE DO CATS BECOME SEXUALLY MATURE?

- This varies from one individual to another, but it also depends upon the breed of cat and the time of year.
- With all these factors to take into account, it is not surprising that anything between four and a half and eighteen months can be considered normal for a cat to mature.
- Oriental breeds, particularly the Burmese, seem to mature earlier, on average, than other cats.

HOW OLD DOES MY CAT NEED TO BE TO HAVE HER FIRST LITTER?

Kittens showing the first signs of sexual gestures in their play behaviour.

- The standard response from a breeder would be that you should allow your queen to mature fully before you let her have a litter, which means that she should be at least one year old.
- The reality for mixed-breed cats is that unless they are kept indoors (which most aren't), they will become pregnant when they first start calling.
- It seems a bit tough for a young queen to have a litter of kittens when she is not much older than they are, but in practice queens seem to manage to cope without any problems.

HOW DO I KNOW MY QUEEN IS 'CALLING'?

- I suspect that once it happens you'll know all about it, although some breeds, such as Persians, tend to be much less vociferous than others.
- Most cats totally change their character when they are in season, becoming extra-affectionate, rolling around on their back, and sticking their bottom into the air when they are stroked over their back. They also howl and scream for a tomcat, hence the term 'calling'.
- Some inexperienced owners think that their kitten has developed severe abdominal cramps and phone their vet in a panic.

- Your cat should be up to date with vaccinations against panleukopaenia, cat flu and feline leukaemia virus.
- It is only natural for the owner of a stud cat to be very wary of infectious diseases, as it is very common for diseases to be spread in this way.
- Most of them will ask for a blood test to be carried out to confirm that the cat is negative for feline leukaemia and immunodeficiency viruses.

WILL MY CAT NEED ANY SPECIAL VACCINATIONS OR BLOOD TESTS BEFORE VISITING A STUD CAT?

HOW OFTEN SHOULD I ALLOW MY QUEEN TO HAVE A LITTER OF KITTENS?

- Feral cats, or domestic ones allowed free access outdoors, will usually have a couple of litters every year. Not only is this exhausting for the queen, but it also amounts to a lot of kittens needing homes.
- It is unlikely that a cat who produces that many litters year after year will live out her full potential life expectancy.
- It is far preferable to allow a cat to recover fully from the effects of carrying and rearing her kittens by just letting her have one litter a year, or even neutering her after her first litter.

HOW CAN I STOP MY QUEEN FROM COMING INTO SEASON?

- There are hormonal preparations, most commonly used in long-acting injectable form, that can be given to cats to prevent them from calling.
- It is not usually advised that they be used to stop a cat from having her first season, however, and they need to be repeated regularly to maintain their effect.
- Most do not interfere with subsequent fertility, but the time between the cessation of treatment and the resumption of calling varies considerably.
- If the intention is not to breed from a cat again, the consensus is that it is better to have a female surgically neutered.

Feral mother cat lying with her kittens, about six weeks old, one still suckling, outside their hollow log nursery.

- It is difficult to draw a hard line between inbreeding, which is essential to establish the desirable and distinctive characteristics of a breed, and over-breeding, in which features are taken to an extreme that interferes with the health of the cat.

- There certainly are examples of over-breeding that are detrimental to the cat. For example, the flattened faces of many Persians make them very prone to eye and respiratory problems. The hairless Sphynx cat is also, arguably, a case of taking breeding skills to an unacceptable extreme, producing a cat that would not survive long in an outdoor environment.

DOES OVER-BREEDING CAUSE HEALTH PROBLEMS?

Persion cat with characteristic flattened face.

Hairless Sphynx cat.

Ten year old farm cat, grown baggy from producing 2–3 litters a year.

mating

How to ensure that your cat mates successfully.

- With a non-pedigree cat that normally goes outdoors, most owners just allow nature to take its course. It's amazing how, even in an area where all the male cats appear to be neutered, some tom always seems to be around to oblige.
- With a pedigree cat the procedure is very different. First, you will obviously have to keep your cat indoors when she is calling. You should be able to obtain a list of stud cat owners from the breed club for your particular breed of cat, or perhaps even by visiting a cat show in your area and talking to experienced breeders.
- Make sure you choose a proven stud who is known to sire healthy, good-quality kittens.

CAN YOU PUT ANY BREEDS TOGETHER FOR MATING?

- You can, but of course they would not be pedigree kittens.
- Many new breeds have been produced by crossbreeding existing ones; among them is the Burmilla, a cross between a Burmese and a Chinchilla.
- But producing a new variety of cat is not as simple as just crossing two breeds together. A breeding programme has to be developed and a standard formulated that states just what the new breed should look like. It takes many years before a new breed is officially recognised by the national and international governing bodies.
- If you wish to experiment by crossing two different breeds, or even producing half-pedigree and half mixed-breed kittens you are free to do so (I have a delightful pair of kittens produced when a Maine Coon female had an unplanned night out on the town), but you cannot sell the kittens as pedigrees.
- However, there is no reason why the pedigree queen should not go on to have perfectly acceptable pedigree litters in the future.

Four breed mixture: Chinchilla and Persian cross with Ragdoll and Turkish Van cross.

Mating may not always be successful.

WHY IS IT THAT MY QUEEN HAS FAILED TO BECOME PREGNANT?

- There are many possible reasons for this, but the most common reasons are:
- **Failure to call**
  Timid queens housed in a group with other intact females may suppress their signs of oestrus. Hormonal disorders also occur, but are very difficult to identify and treat.
- **Failure to mate**
  Uncommon, but may be seen in a nervous queen.
- **Failure to conceive**
  This may be due to hormonal imbalance or even a physical abnormality, with an essential part of the reproductive tract missing.

I WAS SURE THAT MY QUEEN WAS PREGNANT, BUT NO KITTENS APPEARED; WHAT DO YOU SUPPOSE HAPPENED?

- Failure to carry kittens to full term.
- Sometimes foetuses are conceived, but are either resorbed back into the body or aborted out of it. This is commonly due to an infection, particularly with feline leukaemia virus but sometimes with bacteria.
- It may be that she did give birth after a normal term but that problems during labour caused the death of the kittens.

pregnancy

How to ensure your pregnant queen has a healthy, trouble-free pregnancy.

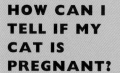

HOW LONG DOES A PREGNANCY LAST?

- The average duration of pregnancy is about 63 days, but anything from 61 to 69 days is considered normal.

HOW CAN I TELL IF MY CAT IS PREGNANT?

- The first change after a successful mating is likely to be some reddening and swelling of the teats.
- By four or five weeks you may well notice that her abdomen has become enlarged and pendulous, and soon she may start to prepare for the arrival of the kittens, seeking out dark corners to make a nest.
- There is no simple blood test that can be carried out to detect pregnancy in a cat, but a vet can usually feel foetal swellings in the uterus by gently palpating her abdomen at three to four weeks' gestation.
- After that, the swellings merge together, and it can be more difficult to confirm pregnancy manually, but ultrasound or radiography can be used to detect the unborn kittens in the later stages if necessary.

Palpating the abdomen of pregnant, blue-eyed, white cat Snowdrop (above). Blue-cream, Burmese-cross Harebell, three days before giving birth to seven kittens (left).

- Yes. If a cat is mated but fertilisation of her eggs does not take place, she will stop calling, as she would if she were pregnant, and usually start calling again five or six weeks later.
- Some cat breeders even keep a vasectomised tomcat to mate with queens that are not needed for breeding to stop them from calling.

CAN CATS HAVE FALSE PREGNANCIES?

- Not much. Whereas hormone treatment can be given to bitches as a form of 'morning-after' treatment to prevent pregnancy, this cannot be done with cats.
- There are drugs that can be used to try to induce an abortion, but there are none that I could confidently say are safe for cats.
- The only course of action guaranteed to prevent your queen from giving birth would be to have her spayed. It is a much bigger operation to remove a womb when it is pregnant than when it is dormant, which makes the surgical risks significantly greater.
- It is probably best to let her have a litter and then have her spayed without delay to make sure the same thing doesn't happen again.

WHAT CAN I DO TO STOP MY PREGNANT CAT FROM HAVING KITTENS?

- You should not allow your cat to be mated if she is not in good body condition at that time.
- Pregnant queens build up body fat and gain weight steadily throughout their pregnancy, so from the time of mating onwards she can be fed on a high-energy food.
- A cat food that is designed for feeding kittens is also likely to be suitable for feeding pregnant queens. As her womb gets significantly larger in the second half of pregnancy, she will prefer to eat little and often. Feeding a complete dry kitten food is ideal for this, as it can be left out for her to help herself.
- The same diet can be fed throughout lactation and can also be fed—softened with water—to kittens when they are weaned.

HOW SHOULD I FEED MY CAT DURING HER PREGNANCY?

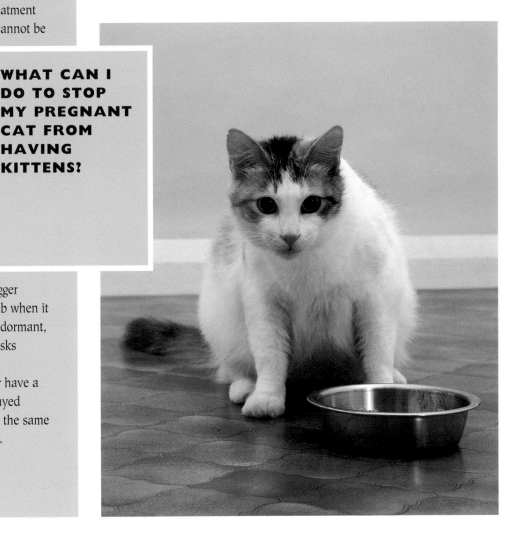

IS IT SAFE TO GIVE A QUEEN MEDICATION DURING PREGNANCY?

- Just as with humans, it is best to avoid giving any medication that is not strictly necessary during pregnancy, and then to use only drugs that are known to be harmless to the unborn foetuses.
- Do not under any circumstances give any proprietary medicines or those prescribed for other animals.

- Cat aerobics are definitely 'out' during the later stages of pregnancy, but pregnant queens are generally very sensible about what they should and should not do, and damage to unborn kittens through violent exercise is very rare.
- Just take a commonsense approach, and do what you can to discourage your cat from jumping around excessively.

MY QUEEN IS PREGNANT. SHOULD SHE BE EXERCISING?

birth

What happens when your cat gives birth and how you can help.

WHAT DO I NEED TO HAVE ON HAND WHEN MY CAT GIVES BIRTH?

- Well before your queen goes into labour, you should encourage her to use a suitable nesting box. A large cardboard box lined with paper will do fine and can be discarded and replaced when it gets soiled, but more elaborate wooden ones can be made or bought.
- You need to be prepared to cope if the mother decides she wants nothing to do with her kittens:
- Hot water bottle to keep the kittens warm.
- Antiseptic cream. Use one that is safe for cats, such as Savlon.
- Bowl for warm water.
- Cotton thread to tie off the umbilical cord if the queen does not bite it.
- Scissors.
- Sterile gauze swabs.
- Cotton wool.
- Milk substitute and feeding bottle.
- Prepare well in advance to avoid any last-minute panic, in case you find you need to hand-rear the kittens when the shops are closed.

HOW WILL I KNOW WHEN MY CAT IS ABOUT TO GIVE BIRTH?

● She will become restless and look for a dark corner in which to hide.

● As labour starts, she will breathe more rapidly, and there may be some vaginal discharge. This will be clear at first but may become bloody as the birth process progresses.

● Contractions will then start, initially perhaps once an hour, but increasing to about every 30 seconds before the first kitten is born.

● The fluid-filled amniotic sac will appear first; it may be passed with the kitten inside, or it may rupture and follow the kitten with the placenta.

● It is not abnormal or unusual for kittens to be born with their hind feet first.

1 *Burmese-cross kitten, Red, being born tail-first.*

2 *Red, waiting for his placenta to come away.*

3 *Red, newly born but still wet, with two of his older siblings.*

4 *Mother cat, Pansy, suckling her six newborn kittens, now clean and dry.*

- Whatever elaborate arrangements you have made, cats will often not cooperate with your plans, and many a litter has been born in a cupboard or on a bed.
- Don't stress your cat by trying to force her to give birth where you want her to.
- However, you should keep her indoors with a litter tray to avoid the possibility of her giving birth out-of-doors.

WHERE SHOULD MY CAT HAVE HER KITTENS?

WHAT ARE THE DANGER SIGNS THAT LABOUR IS GOING WRONG?

- Fortunately, problems during the process of giving birth are relatively rare in cats.
- Overzealous supervision of a cat in labour may serve only to inhibit her and cause complications, so keep a watchful eye from a distance if you can.
- In the late stages of pregnancy it is normal for a cat to appear restless, but a green or red discharge from the vulva without any other signs of labour may indicate a problem and should be checked out by a vet.
- Once the delivery of the kittens begins, it is normal for there to be a considerable gap between kittens, but if the queen is straining hard for more than an hour without success, it could be a sign that a kitten is stuck in the birth canal.
- Similarly, if a queen tires and ceases to strain at all, obviously appearing restless and exhausted, it could indicate uterine inertia—in which the womb is failing to contract. Sometimes a vet will be able to get the birth process going normally again, but a Caesarean section is often needed once problems develop because the relatively small size of the cat makes any manual assistance very difficult.

- Be ready to help if there are problems, but your involvement during a normal birth process should be minimal. Some very domesticated cats do seem to want the assurance of having their owners close by, but this is unusual.
- Watch from a distance and avoid the temptation to interfere.
- If the queen is inexperienced and does not lick the kittens as they are born to remove the amniotic sac, especially from their face and mouth, you should intervene to assist and ensure that the kittens are able to breathe freely.

SHOULD I BE READY TO HELP MY CAT DURING THE BIRTH PROCESS?

WHAT IS ECLAMPSIA, AND HOW CAN IT BE PREVENTED?

- Also called puerperal or lactation tetany, this can occur during late pregnancy or, commonly, after the kittens are born.
- It is caused by a calcium deficiency in the blood due to the amounts of calcium that are being used up to produce milk. Initially it shows itself in restlessness, panting and then in muscle twitching, but it can lead to convulsions and death.
- Although it is essential to make sure that cats receive normal levels of calcium during pregnancy (fresh meat can be very low in this mineral), feeding extra calcium supplements may make the problem worse rather than better. Affected queens must receive calcium injections from a vet without delay, and if necessary, the kittens may need to be weaned early.

cat & new kittens

How to care for your cat and her new litter of kittens.

- Encourage your cat to play the good mother. If that fails, you either have to find a foster mother or face many interrupted nights feeding them with kitten replacement milk from a kitten feeding bottle every two hours.
- Do not try to rear kittens on cow's milk. Three parts evaporated milk to one part boiled water can be used in an emergency, until balanced milk substitute is obtained. Administer it with an eyedropper.

SHOULD KITTENS WITH CONGENITAL PROBLEMS BE PUT TO SLEEP?

- This is a controversial question, and the answer obviously depends upon the degree of deformity in any particular case.
- If a kitten has an abnormality that will interfere with its normal way of life, it should be put to sleep by a vet as soon as the problem has been recognised.
- Certainly, kittens with congenital abnormalities should not be used for breeding, because many congenital problems are hereditary and will be passed on to future generations.
- If a queen produces more than just a very occasional deformity—ones that could be hereditary rather than developmental—she should not be used for breeding.

WHAT CAN I DO IF MY CAT ATTACKS HER KITTENS?

- The maternal instinct is very strong in cats, and it is astonishing how a young queen who has never given birth before usually knows exactly what to do to care for her young.
- Occasionally, though, this process does not function normally. Most often, the reluctant mother just ignores her young, but sometimes she may turn upon them and, given the chance, kill and even eat them.
- Just what triggers this response is not known, but it is more likely in a highly strung cat who behaves this way under stress. She should be checked over by a vet to make sure there is no medical reason for her behaviour.
- There is a chance that some tranquillising medication may help, but often the only way to save the kittens is to keep them away from their mother and to either foster or hand-rear them.

MY CAT PICKS UP HER KITTENS VERY ROUGHLY. IS SHE LIKELY TO HURT THEM?

- No. It's perfectly normal for a queen to pick up her kittens by the scruff of their necks, but sometimes she may take their whole head into her mouth.
- The kittens have a reflex reaction in which they go limp and passive when picked up in this way so that their mother is able to move them around.

HOW SOON SHOULD I HANDLE MY NEW KITTENS?

- Recent studies have shown that the early experiences of a kitten, from as young as two weeks, play a vital role in forming the character of the adult cat.
- By seven weeks, much of the shaping has been completed, and it is then much more difficult to modify their subsequent behaviour. Therefore, plenty of stroking and handling of even very young kittens is vital if they are to grow into sociable cats.
- At two weeks of age their eyes are barely open and their movements uncoordinated, but their senses of smell and hearing are well developed, and they will quickly learn to appreciate the sound and smell of human contact, even if only for a few minutes at a time.

Checking the umbilical cord on a day-old kitten (above) and gentle handling at one week old (right).

HOW DO I WEAN KITTENS ONTO SOLID FOOD?

- Get the kittens used to lapping milk substitute from a bowl first. You can do this by getting them to lick milk off your finger and then putting your finger into the bowl.
- You can then gradually thicken the consistency of the milk with some toast.
- You may even find that kittens will lick mashed-up tinned kitten food off your finger and then take to licking it from a bowl.
- This process can be started at around five weeks of age.

Five-week old kittens learning from their mother.

FOR HOW LONG SHOULD A KITTEN STAY WITH ITS MOTHER?

- There is some dispute about this, as many pedigree cat breeders insist on keeping their kittens until they have completed their vaccination course at 12 weeks of age, whereas many animal behaviourists believe that it is preferable to move a kitten into its new home as soon as it is fully weaned from its mother.
- It's certainly normal practice to re-home non-pedigree kittens at seven or eight weeks of age, and there is no reason to treat pedigrees differently, as long as they are kept isolated from any possible source of infection until they have completed a full course of injections.
- If pedigree kittens are being kept penned in a non-domestic environment, there is a strong incentive to get them homed well before 12 weeks of age.

IS IT POSSIBLE FOR KITTENS TO PICK UP INFECTIOUS DISEASES FROM THEIR MOTHER?

- Yes. Although the mother is a great source of warmth, food and comfort, she is also a major potential source of infection for her kittens.
- Roundworms, ear mites and fleas are all commonly passed on to future generations in this way, but fortunately we have drugs to treat these conditions that are safe and effective in even the youngest cats.
- Viral infections can be more of a problem. As protection against viruses, kittens obtain antibodies from their mother, particularly in the colostrum, which is the milk she produces in the first two days after their birth. This protects them up to around eight weeks of age, but around that time they may succumb to viruses that their mother may be excreting, such as feline leukaemia virus, feline coronavirus and the cat flu viruses.
- When this happens in the litter of a queen kept in a cattery with other breeding queens, it may be necessary to keep the litter with their mother isolated from all other cats from birth, and then wean them early, at about six weeks of age, and keep them isolated from all other cats from that time, including their mother.

HOW CAN I
FIND GOOD
HOMES FOR
MY KITTENS?

- You really should consider this before you decide to breed from your cat, rather than find homes once the kittens have arrived.
- There is usually a strong demand for pedigree kittens, and you can advertise in one of the specialist magazines that you have a litter available. Most cat clubs also keep a register of litters for their particular breed which is passed on to any inquirers.
- Non-pedigree kittens can be more of a problem. Many people wish to keep one or two kittens themselves and have enough contacts through friends and relatives to be able to find good homes for the rest of the litter (four to five is an average number, but a first litter often contains fewer kittens).
- You could try putting up a notice in your local veterinary clinic. Do not place them with retail outlets, because you should approve the homes to which your kitten will go. Many pet shop owners who refuse to sell kittens do keep a list of those needing homes.

HOW CAN I TELL THE SEX OF MY KITTENS?

- This is not as easy as it may sound in very young kittens, but the task is made easier if you compare two kittens of different sexes side by side.
- The female has a vertical slit-shaped genital opening just below the anus, whereas in the male the opening is round and further from the anus.
- As the male kitten matures, the testicles can be seen developing in the gap between the anus and the prepuce (the skin that covers the penis), so that the difference becomes obvious. It is at this stage that quite a few owners have to change their cat's name from Georgina to George!

Female.

Male.

spaying & neutering

The arguments for and against having your cat neutered or spayed.

- To a certain extent, but we can't pretend that the way we keep domestic cats is 'natural' anyway.
- Female cats living a feral existence just become kitten factories, and males have a very tough time maintaining their place in the hierarchy.
- A tom-cat may do well if he rises to a prime position in his area, but other cats will show no mercy when he begins to flag.
- Cats that live a 'natural' life must struggle to survive, and they tend to die at a much earlier age than the average pet.

ISN'T IT UNNATURAL TO NEUTER A CAT?

SHOULD I HAVE MY CAT NEUTERED?

- Yes. Unless you are going to breed from your cat, you should definitely have your cat spayed.
- In the case of female cats this is primarily to prevent unwanted litters or the exhaustion caused by a female's continual and fruitless calling, but it will also prevent womb infections and breast cancer from developing later in life.
- Male cats make much better pets if they are neutered. If they are not, they produce very strong-smelling urine, which they then spray around their territory as a marker to deter other cats. They will try to establish a large territory, often roaming off for days to patrol their boundaries and fight off any other male cats.

WHEN SHOULD I NEUTER MY PET?

- You should consult your vet and take his or her advice on this matter, as the policy differs from practice to practice.
- A female cat should be spayed before she starts calling, at above five months. A male cat should be neutered at five and a half to six months, before he is likely to develop any undesirable male-related behaviour.

WHY HASN'T NEUTERING STOPPED MY MALE CAT FROM FIGHTING?

- Neutered male cats will still fight to defend their territory from other male cats, but they will generally be satisfied with establishing a much smaller area of land and will be more tolerant of other cats encroaching on it.
- We ask a lot of male domestic cats in suburban areas by expecting them to live together happily at a much higher feline density than they would encounter in a natural situation.

CAN MALE CATS HAVE A VASECTOMY INSTEAD OF CASTRATION?

- It is possible, and some breeders use vasectomised males to mate with their queens to stop them from calling when a pregnancy is undesirable.
- Although the operation (which involves cutting the tubes that carry sperm from the testes to the penis) will make a tom-cat infertile, he will still develop all the secondary male characteristics such as fighting and urine spraying.
- It is not an advisable option for a pet male cat. The procedure still requires anaesthesia and a certain degree of expertise that makes it more expensive than regular castration.

IF MY CAT IS NEUTERED WILL HE STILL BE ABLE TO DEFEND HIMSELF?

- Yes. Although he will not fight as ferociously or try to defend such a large territory as would an intact tom-cat, he should still be well able to look after himself, at least vis-à-vis other neutered cats.
- Tom-cats develop very thick skin and strong musculature, and can cause havoc in a suburban area. If there is an unneutered tom-cat causing problems, you could try to contact his owners and encourage them to take him to their vet; or if you are confident he is feral, you could arrange with a cat rescue organisation to have him trapped and neutered.

- No. This old wives' tale without any foundation in fact has allowed many unwanted kittens to be born.
- If you want the experience of rearing a litter, or perhaps want one of your cat's offspring to continue the line, and you have thought carefully about homing the rest of the litter, go right ahead.
- If not, have your cat spayed before her first season; the operation is less traumatic when the womb is immature, and, moreover, there is then no risk of an unwanted pregnancy.

ISN'T IT BEST TO ALLOW MY CAT TO HAVE ONE LITTER BEFORE SHE IS SPAYED?

HOW SOON AFTER GIVING BIRTH SHOULD MY CAT BE SPAYED?

- Cats can start to call again very soon after they have given birth, although generally they will not begin to do so while they are still feeding their kittens.
- You should watch your cat closely for any signs of coming into season, and keep her confined indoors if necessary.
- I would advise spaying as soon as the milk has dried up, usually about two weeks after the kittens have been weaned.

WHAT DOES THE SPAYING OPERATION INVOLVE?

- The procedure, technically known as an ovaro-hysterectomy, involves removing both ovaries and the womb.
- Your cat will need to be taken to your veterinarian in the morning, having been kept in overnight and having eaten no food since the night before. You will be given preoperative and postoperative instructions, so follow them closely and contact the veterinarian's office or clinic if you are not sure what to do.
- The anesthetic may be given by injection, or sometimes initially by injection followed by gas. If it is given intravenously, your cat will probably have some hair clipped off her foreleg.
- The operation is done via a midline incision. The incision is usually a very small one, requiring only two or three sutures, and most practices allow their patients to go home the same day.
- Feed only a light diet for the first 24 hours, and keep her indoors until given the all-clear by your veterinarian.
- Sutures are generally removed seven to ten days after the operation, by which time most cats are behaving as if nothing had happened.

MUST MY CAT BE KEPT INDOORS AFTER HER SPAYING OPERATION?

- Unless there are complicating factors, the incision for a routine spaying operation is very small. Also there is very little pressure on the wound from within the abdomen.
- Your veterinarian will know your own cat's particular circumstances, and you should follow the advice you are given, but after a completely routine operation, your spayed cat can start going outdoors again after a few days.
- Some procedures may require a much longer period of restriction.

WILL SHE STOP CALLING AFTER SHE HAS BEEN SPAYED?

- Yes. Because both ovaries and the uterus are usually removed, she should no longer come into season and will stop calling.
- Some queens seem to produce female hormones after the operation, and in very rare cases will continue to call, but there is no danger that they are fertile.

A young cat relaxing and grooming after her spaying operation. Keep a check on her sutures to ensure they do not become infected, especially if she licks them a lot.

We ask a lot of our pet cats by putting them into a domestic environment and expecting them to forget all their wild instincts. We must seem such strangely behaved creatures to them—we sleep all through the night, we cover ourselves in strange scents to mask our natural body odours, and we shriek with disgust when brought a present of a juicy mouse. In many ways, the dog is more naturally inclined to settle into a life of domestication. Its wild counterparts naturally live and hunt in packs, and it is a relatively small step for a dog to consider the resident humans as its pack. Provided that a dog understands its place in the social hierarchy, it can readily settle down as a pet.

The closest wild relatives of our domestic cat are individualistic by nature, and the domestic cat still remains very much a 'wild cat' at heart. Whereas many other species have been selectively bred for thousands of years, it is only in very recent times that humans have

9 Behaviour

significantly interfered with the physical form and, to a lesser extent, the temperament of the cat.

By learning more about the development of the cat from a wild animal to one that has learned to live with humans, we can better understand some of those puzzling aspects of feline behaviour. For this chapter is not just about behaviour, but also misbehaviour. Some behaviour that we find unacceptable is, in fact, natural and normal; an obvious example is urine marking. Other problems may be neurotic behaviour patterns, caused by a combination of genetic influences (these problems are more common in certain breeds such as the Siamese) and the stresses of living in a modern domestic environment. An apartment in the centre of a city could not be further removed from the semi-desert wilderness of northern Africa from which our domestic cat migrated more than 4,000 years ago.

cat culture

Understanding the way that your cat reacts to the world around it.

CAN CATS SEE IN THE DARK?

- No, but their eyes are well adapted to seeing in low light levels to enable them to hunt in the evenings and the early morning.
- The cat has slit-like pupils that can open widely to let in as much light as possible, and the light sensitive layer at the back of the eye has a reflective layer behind it, so that the light beams are reflected back into the eye and their effect is magnified.
- This is why cats' eyes glow in the dark when a bright light, such as a car headlight, is reflected out of the eyes.

DO CATS SEE IN COLOUR?

- Cats have very poor colour vision. We know this from examination of the cat's retina, which is at the back of the eye.
- In cats, as in humans, the retina contains two kinds of light receptors: rods, which detect only black, white and shades of gray; and cones, which are able to distinguish different colours.
- Rods are much better than cones at seeing in low light levels. At dusk, when colours progressively fade into shades of gray, the rods come into their own. It is at this time of day, and at dawn, that cats do their hunting, for this is when their prey are most likely to be moving about.
- Because rods are much better than cones at detecting movement (cones are better at fine detail), it is not surprising that the cat's retina consists almost entirely of rods; these are the light receptors that enabled its wild ancestors to survive.

Tabby-tortoiseshell cat with dilated pupils in low light (above left) and with pupils closed to slits in bright light (left).

- Whiskers are long, modified hairs with many nerve endings at the base. Muscles move them in groups. They are very sensitive to touch and greatly assist the cat when hunting in the dark.

- A cat carrying a small rodent will wrap its whiskers around it to sense any movement. The whiskers help in the kill, enabling the cat to detect the exact spot in the neck of its prey to insert its canine teeth and dislocate the vertebrae.
- If its whiskers have been removed, it is still capable of catching its victim, but cannot accurately kill it with one bite.

- Cats have a highly specialised nervous system which is able to orient the body rapidly into the best position for landing during a fall.
- The vestibular apparatus, which is the organ of balance deep within the ear, is able to detect which way up the cat should be, and the head will rotate into a horizontal position. The supple spine then twists to bring the body into alignment with the head, and the forelegs stretch out, ready to absorb the impact of landing.
- Cats have been known to survive falls from multi-storey buildings, but injuries to the pelvis and limbs are common.

- Another injury that often results from a fall is a broken lower jaw; this is caused by a five-point landing, in which all four feet hit the ground, followed by the chin.

After falling a short distance, a cat rights itself.

SHOULD I PUT MY CAT OUT AT NIGHT?

- No. Cats are actually crepuscular creatures, not nocturnal, which means that they are most active at dusk and dawn.
- Like humans, they like to curl up in a warm spot at night, so if there is no cat flap they should be let out at breakfast time and then kept indoors as darkness approaches, safe from harm.
- Cats generally seem to adapt surprisingly well to our human daily rhythms, and most will happily remain active when their owners return home and then curl up to sleep in the evenings.

- I think the official answer has to be no, but I must admit that many nights I have to fight for space on my bed among two or three of my five cats.
- Even cats that have access to the outdoors will usually come in during the night for a snooze, and what warmer and more comfortable spot can there be than the owner's bed?
- This is certainly not advisable for anyone suffering from asthma, however, and excessive amounts of dander (dead skin cells) in the bedroom may trigger an attack.
- You should also make sure that your cats are kept in tip-top health, and especially that your preventive flea control is up-to-date, or you may be troubled by some very itchy flea bites from overly close proximity to your cat.

SHOULD I ALLOW MY CAT TO SLEEP ON MY BED?

**MY CAT LOVES
TO SUCK ON
WOOL, AND
EVEN BITES
CHUNKS OUT
OF MY
SWEATER.
WHY DOES HE
DO THIS, AND
CAN IT BE
HARMFUL?**

- It is not uncommon for young cats to suck on fabric as a form of comfort, and although this can be a bit disconcerting, it is not generally harmful.
- However, some cats take this a step further and actually start eating fabric, particularly wool. It is not known why they do this, but it is especially common in Siamese and Burmese cats.
- It can lead to serious problems, not only leaving your clothes looking as if a whole squadron of moths had attacked them, but sometimes causing obstruction of the cat's intestine.
- The habit should certainly be discouraged, and it is a good incentive to keep your bedroom very tidy with all clothes cleared away into wardrobes and cupboards.
- There is some evidence to suggest that increasing the fibre levels in the diet may help to reduce the desire to eat fabric.

**WHY DOES MY
CAT GO
CRAZY OVER
CATNIP?**

- It's funny stuff, catnip (*Nepeta cataria*). For us humans, and for some cats, it does nothing at all. But some cats get very excited about it. They will approach the plant, sniff it, lick it, bite it and roll around in it, all with increasing enthusiasm; some cats even leap into the air.
- All the signs suggest that catnip is having a hallucinogenic effect, but fortunately for cats, this 'trip' seems to last for only about ten minutes and is not thought to have any undesirable side effects.
- The plant is a member of the mint family and contains an oil called hepetalactone, which is the active compound that causes the behavioural reaction in many cats. Manufacturers of cat toys have taken advantage of this by incorporating the compound into some of their products.
- You should avoid planting catnip in the middle of your most prized flower bed if you don't want to encourage cats to treat it as a playground.

cat talk

How your cat communicates with you and how to interpret what it is trying to tell you.

DO CATS COMMUNICATE WITH HUMANS?

- Yes. Of course, they can't use speech, but cats have a rich repertoire of sounds and body language that they can use.
- Studies of cat behaviour have shown that they tend to use a totally different language for communicating with people from the one they use with other cats—perhaps they think that humans are too stupid to understand true 'cat-ese'!
- They adapt what they say to how we respond, so that if we respond in a positive way to a certain sound, they are much more likely to use it again. Some cats even develop specific sounds that they use only for a certain member of the family.
- We recognise about 16 different vocalisations in cats, although there are probably many more subtle variations that we are unable to differentiate.
- Some breeds, particularly Oriental-type cats such as the Siamese, are especially vocal.

- Who can be sure about what is going on inside the mind of a cat?
- All the evidence suggests that cats are not able to understand our verbal communications as such, but they certainly can respond to individual words. More importantly, they are very sensitive to our body language, and can respond to what we are feeling, and even anticipate what we are about to do.
- It often seems that cats are better at understanding what we are thinking than what we are saying.

CAN CATS UNDERSTAND WHAT THEIR OWNERS ARE SAYING?

Frightened cat

Curious cat

HOW DO CATS COMMUNICATE WITH EACH OTHER?

- When it comes to communicating with each other rather than humans, cats employ an even larger vocabulary of sounds, postures and scents.
- Purring starts at a very early age as a means of communication between a mother and her kittens. The distressed yowl of a kitten that has become separated from its mother is obvious to anyone.
- A range of miaows serve for ordinary feline conversation; but when a cat is angry, a growl, or even a hiss, is used to warn off the opposition. A female cat in season is described as 'calling' because she does just that, emitting loud yowls that not only wake up the whole neighbourhood but announce to tom-cats far and wide that she is ready for mating.
- For cats, non-verbal communication is every bit as important as the verbal kind. The cat that is frightened will flatten its ears, stand on tiptoe and puff itself up as large as possible, with its hair literally standing on end, to make itself look large and intimidating. Sometimes it will even adopt a sideways stance to increase its apparent size. The eyes, ears and facial expression are particularly important in feline communications:
- Frightened cat—ears folded down, pupils dilated.
- Curious cat—ears forward and pupils slightly dilated.
- Contented cat—ears erect, eyes half-closed and pupils slit-like. A long, slow blink is a sign of recognition.
- Aggressive cat—ears forward, pupils dilated and teeth bared as a warning.

Contented cat

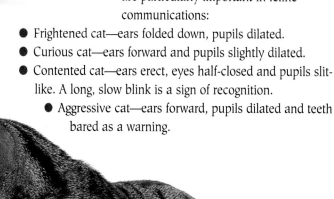

Aggressive cat

- If you look at a cat's head face-on, you will notice that the hair below the ears is thinner than elsewhere. This is because besides hair follicles, these areas have a rich supply of scent-secreting glands which secrete something known as a pheromone. This is a type of hormone; but instead of working in the bloodstream, it is active as molecules in the air.

- Cats are very sensitive to these airborne hormones, and even have a small sac called Jacobson's organ high up in the roof of the mouth to detect them. This is why you may see your cat making a strange sniffing expression, with the head held high and the mouth slightly open to draw air into this organ; this expression is known as the flehmen reaction.

- Pheromones play an important part in sexual and territorial behaviour in cats, and studies show that human pheromones have a strong subconscious effect upon our sexual behaviour.

- By rubbing its cheek against objects, including your ankles, the cat is sharing its scent with you, and feels at ease when you are around.

- This fact has been utilised in sprays made of cat pheromone extracts that can be used to help relax a cat in unfamiliar surroundings. Surprisingly, these artificial pheromones do not encourage your cat to spray.

WHY DOES MY CAT RUB HIS FACE AGAINST MY LEG?

WHY DO CATS PURR?

- Although we assume that cats purr when they are contented, experience shows that they also purr at other times when this is not the case. For example, vets often hear badly injured cats, obviously in pain, purring on the consulting room table.

- The purr originates in early kittenhood as a means of communication between kittens and their mother to signify that all is well, particularly during feeding. The sound is unusual in that the distinctive whirring noise can be made with each outward breath, as well as each inward one, even with the mouth closed, for hours on end.

- It seems that the purr is used to signal a friendly social mood, and can be used as a plea for assistance in times of stress, as well as a sign of contentment when the cat is completely relaxed.

- The kneading action of the cat's paws is exactly the same as that performed by kittens when they are suckling from their mother. In that situation, the massaging action helps to stimulate the mammary glands to produce a flow of milk, and the kitten's mouth waters, or salivates, in anticipation of the meal that is to come.

WHY DOES MY CAT FLEX ITS CLAWS AND DRIBBLE WHEN ON MY LAP?

- Adult cats tend to have a kitten-mother relationship with their owners and often behave in ways similar to their behaviour when young. When the cat is lying on its owner's lap, extremely relaxed and contented, it must recall the happy times spent suckling from its mother, and so it instinctively goes through the motions of stimulating the milk supply.
- I'm afraid you just have to feel flattered and ignore the soggy clothes and claw-pricked skin.

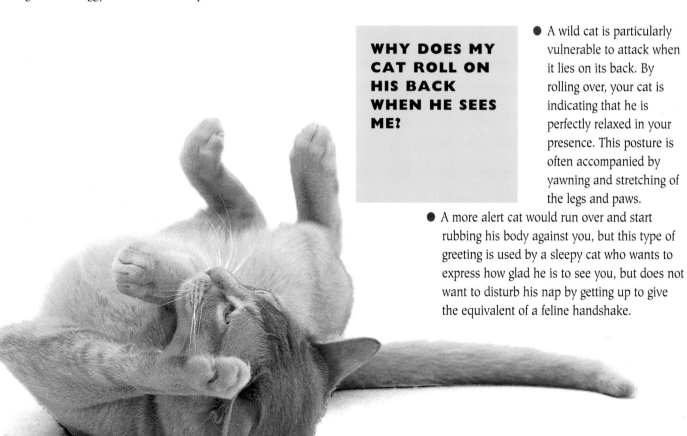

WHY DOES MY CAT ROLL ON HIS BACK WHEN HE SEES ME?

- A wild cat is particularly vulnerable to attack when it lies on its back. By rolling over, your cat is indicating that he is perfectly relaxed in your presence. This posture is often accompanied by yawning and stretching of the legs and paws.
- A more alert cat would run over and start rubbing his body against you, but this type of greeting is used by a sleepy cat who wants to express how glad he is to see you, but does not want to disturb his nap by getting up to give the equivalent of a feline handshake.

- A dog wags its tail when it is happy, but in cats this indicates a quite different mood.
- Tail wagging is a sign of internal conflict in cats—they are unable to make up their minds about how to react to some kind of stimulus.
- Thus, a cat who is waiting to pounce on its prey will often stay perfectly still, except for its wagging tail, which indicates that it is trying to make up its mind as to when the time is right. Similarly, if you are stroking a cat and it starts to wag its tail, this might be a sign that it is unsure whether it is still enjoying itself, so it may be time for you to stop.

WHAT DOES IT MEAN WHEN A CAT WAGS ITS TAIL?

HOW CAN ONE PREVENT THE GRIEVING OF OTHER CATS IN THE HOUSEHOLD WHEN ONE CAT DIES OR IS PUT DOWN?

- We cannot know whether a cat realises that another cat has died, but they certainly do notice a change in their normal routine.
- They may become restless, lose interest in their food, search around the house for the missing cat, and even start to mutilate themselves. In severe cases, veterinary treatment with stress-reducing drugs may be necessary.
- However, the remaining cat's reaction is not always negative: sometimes a cat that has been living in the 'shadow' of another may come out of its shell, becoming much more extroverted and affectionate.
- Some people believe that if a cat is shown the body of its dead companion it will realise that it has died and will be better able to come to terms with the loss. I am not convinced that this is true, but it is unlikely to do any harm.

Red tabby cat, Georgie, flicking tail and looking angry.

Red tabby cat, Georgie, with tail up being friendly.

cat reform

How to understand your cat's behaviour and modify it if necessary.

HOW CAN I STOP MY CAT FROM CLIMBING THE CURTAINS?

- The facile answer to this question is to suggest that you get blinds instead. For a less expensive alternative, try some mild aversion therapy. Just a clap of the hands, or a short, sharp blast with a water pistol in more extreme cases, should deter your cat from this kind of behaviour.
- Make sure the cat is not aware that you are responsible for the mild punishment, or it will quickly learn to misbehave only when you are not around.

HOW CAN I PUNISH MY CAT WHEN SHE MISBEHAVES?

- Punishment is not generally a very good way of modifying your cat's behaviour, particularly if the cause is stress-related, for you will just make your cat more stressed. It is far preferable to find a way of redirecting that behaviour so that it no longer poses a problem, or removing the underlying cause.
- However, there are times when aversion therapy is the only means of dealing with a problem. With this method the cat learns to associate some unpleasant event with the undesirable behaviour. A water spray, such as from a water pistol, is ideal for this, as it can be used at a distance, and is completely harmless, yet is something that most cats find quite unpleasant.
- It is important that the cat cannot see you actually using the spray, or it will simply learn to misbehave when you are not around. It has to be like a 'bolt from the blue' which strikes just as the cat carries out the dastardly deed. There is absolutely no point in punishing your cat after the event.
- You will therefore need plenty of patience to 'stake out' your cat from a suitable hiding place. Needless to say, you should avoid whooping gleefully when you catch your cat in the act and successfully administer the penalty.

- Cats need to scratch at something firm with their claws in order to pull off the dead outer layer of nail, leaving the new, sharp one that has grown underneath to replace it. This activity also exercises and strengthens the extraction and protrusion apparatus of the claws, which is vital to allow the cat to catch its prey, climb trees and defend itself.

- But scratching also has another significant function in cats. The skin between their toes contains a large number of scent-secreting glands, and the scratching squeezes out the scent from the glands and onto the fabric, acting as a form of territory marker. Fabric will absorb this scent well, which is why it is preferred to leather or wood by many cats.

- Make sure that your cat has some alternative scratching post available—perhaps made out of a similar fabric attached to a piece of wood. The scratching post must be firmly attached to the wall or some other heavy object, so that the cat can tug on it without it moving.

- Some commercial scratching posts impregnated with catnip may attract the cat's attention more effectively. If you can isolate your cat from your furnishings, this will help to break the habit; or you could purchase one of the cat pheromone sprays which mimic the effect of the cat's scent and thus reduce their need to impregnate the fabric themselves.

- As a last resort, you may have to use aversion therapy with a water spray, but remember that it is essential that you spray the cat only if you catch him in the act, and make sure that he does not realise it is you doing the spraying.

- De-clawing is a painful procedure that should not be carried out on cats, especially if they venture outdoors.

MY CAT IS RUINING MY FURNITURE. WHAT SHOULD I DO?

I KEEP HAVING TO GET MY CAT DOWN FROM A TREE. HE JUST SITS UP THERE AND WAILS. HOW CAN I STOP HIM CLIMBING IT?

- I would make very sure that your cat really is stuck before trying to rescue him. Although going up is often easier for a cat than getting down again, most cats can eventually manage it if left to their own resources.

- Your cat has probably learned that by sitting up in the tree and yowling he can attract a great deal of your attention, and he probably enjoys watching your antics as you try to get him down.

- Apart from taking a very relaxed attitude, there is nothing you can do to stop him from going up in the first place.

HOW CAN I STOP MY CAT FROM DECIMATING THE LOCAL WILDLIFE?

- Not very easily, I'm afraid. You must understand that the main reason that we ever kept cats in the first place was their superb hunting ability. From the cat's point of view, it's a bit tough if we now turn around and say we want them to leave rodents and birds alone.

- Cats kill mainly mice and voles and occasionally a bird, usually one that is already injured or diseased. It's a matter of survival of the fittest, and the species concerned reproduce in large numbers to allow for the fact that only a small minority will survive to breed.

- There is no evidence that the quantity or variety of wildlife is decreasing in suburban areas where cats are allowed to hunt.

- You could try putting a bell on its collar, but most cats seem fairly uninhibited by them.

CAN I TRAIN MY CAT TO DO TRICKS?

- Cats can learn to do tricks, but I find it hard to understand why any cat lover would want to bother to do this.

- Although not nearly as responsive to training as dogs, cats can be taught to follow simple commands such as 'No', 'Down' and 'Here' if you use food treats to reinforce the desired behaviour. But most cat owners admire the cat's independent nature, and do not want to see it behaving out of character.

- The reverse, however, is not true. Most cats are very good at training their owners to respond to commands such as 'Feed me' and 'Open that door (quickly)'.

elimination problems

How to retrain your cat if it starts showing antisocial behaviour either indoors or outside.

WHY DO CATS BURY THEIR FAECES?

- It is always assumed that this is because of the cat's fastidious cleanliness. The truth is less genteel.
- In feral colonies of cats, the dominant tom-cats do not bury their faeces. On the contrary, they pile them up and use them as territory markers to let other cats know they are the bosses. The subordinate members of the group bury their faeces to mask their smell and to avoid challenging the status of the dominant tom-cats.
- Fortunately, cats living in a domestic situation generally accept their subordinate status and cover up their faeces in the litter tray.

MY NEIGHBOUR GETS VERY UPSET ABOUT MY CATS MESSING ON HER LAWN. IS THERE ANYTHING I CAN DO?

- This subject does seem to inflame passions in many neighbourhoods. If you don't wish to keep your cat indoors, you, or the neighbour, might consider purchasing chemical cat deterrents to sprinkle on the ground.
- Crushed mothballs or citrus peelings can be used, as cats dislike the smell. Obviously, you should discourage your neighbours from planting catnip, which will attract cats to their garden.
- Electronic cat deterrents can also be purchased; these emit an ultrasonic noise when they detect movement in the garden, but they are quite expensive.
- I have even heard of people that have gone to a zoo to collect lion dung to spread in their garden—it is said that one sniff of that is enough to strike terror into the heart of any domestic cat!

- This is one of the most common behavioural problems in cats, and is caused by the cat's fulfilling its natural desire to mark its territory. It is most commonly done by males, but females will also sometimes spray.
- If the cat is an intact tom, neutering should be considered. Not only are toms much more inclined to mark their territory than females are, but their urine has a particularly strong smell which is almost impossible to remove.
- Urine spraying is especially common in multi-cat households; in fact, the more cats in a house, the more chance there is of at least one of the cats starting to spray.
- The behaviour is usually sparked off when a cat feels that its territorial security is threatened. The following actions may help to control the problem:
- Have your cat checked by a vet to ensure that there are no underlying medical problems. If you are able to take a urine sample, this would greatly assist in the investigation.
- Shut off any cat flaps, to prevent other cats entering your home.
- Thoroughly clean the soiled areas, using a commercial pet odour neutraliser.
- Spray the marked sites with a proprietary cat pheromone spray.
- Put feeding bowls with food on those sites, as cats will not spray in their feeding areas.
- Put aluminium foil up against the areas that are being sprayed—the noise of the urine hitting the foil will deter the cat.
- Discuss with your vet the use of mild tranquillising drugs to help break the habit.

MY NEUTERED MALE CAT URINATES AND DEFECATES IN CORNERS. WHAT CAN I DO ABOUT IT?

HOW CAN I STOP MY CAT FROM SPRAYING URINE AROUND THE HOUSE?

MY NINE-MONTH-OLD MALE CAT GOES OUT BUT RUSHES BACK TO USE HIS LITTER. SHOULD I TAKE IT AWAY?

- Inappropriate urination and defecation are rather different in their cause and treatment from urine spraying, as this behaviour is often related to a reluctance to use the available facilities, rather than to territorial marking.
- Whereas sprayed urine will be deposited high against a vertical surface, such as a wall, in this case a puddle or a pile will be found on the floor. The following steps may help to control the problem:
- If you don't have a litter tray indoors, try providing one. Your cat may be getting bullied outdoors and thus not wish to relieve itself there.
- Avoid using any strong-smelling disinfectant in the litter tray, as this may deter the cat.
- Try changing the type of cat litter. Even a change of brand may make a difference. Sprinkle some earth in the tray to make it more appealing.
- Place the tray in a quiet corner, so that the cat does not feel unduly exposed using it. A covered litter tray may also make the cat feel more secure.

- Cats feel particularly vulnerable to attack when they are defecating and he obviously does not feel sufficiently confident to use an outdoor spot yet. If you remove the tray, you may end up with a cat who starts defecating around the house.
- Take it gradually and do not force him. Adding some earth to the tray may help, as may pouring some used cat litter into a corner of the yard that you would like to encourage him to use.

fear & nervousness

How your cat's feelings affect its day-to-day behaviour.

MY CAT IS TIMID AND STAYS INDOORS ALL DAY. HOW CAN I GET HER TO GO OUT?

- Many owners worry about the risks facing their cat out-of-doors and would be only too happy to own a cat that liked to stay at home. It's very likely that other cats in the neighbourhood are attacking her when she encroaches onto what they consider to be their territory.
- If you force her to go outdoors, you will probably end up with a very stressed cat who might develop behavioural problems such as urine marking.
- If she is very nervous, you could discuss with your vet the possibility of putting her on a mild tranquilliser. You could even try a herbal remedy such as skullcap and valerian, which will certainly do no harm and may help to allay her fears.
- If this is not effective, I suggest you just appreciate that you have a cat who enjoys her home comforts.

I CAN'T CUDDLE MY KITTEN. SHE TWISTS AND SCRATCHES UNTIL I PUT HER DOWN. WILL I EVER BE ABLE TO PICK HER UP?

- It's important that kittens be handled as much as possible when they are young, because they become harder to tame as they get older. Kittens that feel insecure when picked up must be gradually and gently acclimatised to it.
- Initially you should pick the kitten up just a few inches from the floor, for just a few seconds.
- This should be repeated frequently each day, with the height and duration gradually increasing, so that the kitten becomes accustomed to the sensation without getting frightened.

- Many people would be only too pleased to own a cat that was happy to stay indoors, away from the traffic and other hazards that face cats in the Big Wide World. I certainly wouldn't advise that you force the matter, or you will just make her more nervous.

- If you are determined to get her outdoors, you could try using food to encourage her. Put it beside the door and gradually move the bowl further and further away as your cat builds up her confidence.

- Don't leave the food unattended, as you may end up attracting other cats into your garden, which would probably just make her more nervous.

HOW CAN I STOP MY CAT FROM BEING SO NERVOUS?

MY 18-MONTH-OLD CAT WON'T GO OUTDOORS AT ALL. HOW CAN I GET HER USED TO IT?

- Early exposure to a wide range of different experiences is the key to growing up as a bold and well-adjusted cat, but your cat is presumably past that stage now.

- You need to identify what is causing your cat stress and try to gradually habituate her to the cause, using patience and plenty of kindness. You may find that a herbal remedy or a mild tranquilliser prescribed by your vet will help.

- If the problem is severe, you could seek the assistance of a pet behavioural counsellor. Yes, there really are psychiatrists for pets!

cat manners

Making sense of your cat's antisocial habits, and how to deal with them.

WHY DOES MY CAT ALWAYS JUMP ONTO THE LAP OF PEOPLE WHO DON'T LIKE CATS?

- Direct eye-to-eye contact is seen as threatening by cats, who will give a blink and then turn away if they wish to avoid a confrontation.
- Someone who dislikes cats will instinctively turn away from them.
- Unfortunately, far from seeing this as hostile, a cat will find it reassuring and therefore feel tempted to jump upon that supposedly friendly person. Either that or cats are just naturally contrary.

WHY IS IT THAT MY CAT DOES NOT LIKE HAVING HER RUMP STROKED? IT SEEMS TO HURT HER.

- Many cats, especially females, seem to be sensitive about their rump area. If it is completely out of character—that is, if she enjoys being stroked elsewhere—you should have her checked over to make sure there is not a veterinary problem, such as a spinal injury.
- If all is normal, her reaction probably relates to feline mating behaviour, in which the female will react angrily to advances by a male cat if she is not ready to mate. She will turn and strike out in response if any approach is made to her rear end.

**WE HAVE TWO
BROTHERS
THAT WERE
INSEPARABLE
BUT NOW
FIGHT ALL THE
TIME. WHAT
CAN WE DO?**

● I assume that they have been neutered—if not, that should be at the top of your agenda. Litter mates usually grow up to be very close, but occasionally sibling rivalry takes over and they start to squabble.

● There is no simple answer, other than trying to prevent situations that cause a conflict. For example, two feeding bowls will help prevent any fights about who is going to eat first.

● Two cats that do not get along together usually avoid each other as much as possible. You will find they will establish their own territories in the house, their own entrances and exits (if possible), and their own sleeping areas.

● Fights will break out only when the system breaks down and face-to-face confrontation becomes unavoidable.

MY CAT IS PURRING ON MY LAP ONE MINUTE AND THEN LASHING OUT AT ME THE NEXT. HOW CAN I STOP HIM?

- This is known as the 'petting and biting syndrome' and is well recognised. We can only guess at the reason, but it seems that cats enjoy the stroking and become relaxed, but then reach a point where they feel trapped and vulnerable by being so close to us, at which point their wild instincts get the better of them and they lash out.
- You can detect the warning signs that this is about to happen: The tail starts to twitch, the purring ceases and the cat's body tenses up. You should immediately stop the petting and put the cat down.
- You can gradually build up your cat's tolerance to the petting over a period of time, stopping the moment you detect any sign of aggression.

- There are many possible causes of chronic vomiting in cats, and a thorough health examination to ensure that there is no specific underlying cause is recommended, as is a change of diet (see page 58).
- It may be significant that your cat is frequently sick when you have guests, as some highly strung cats can suffer from a condition known as psychogenic vomiting, which means that the problem is stress-related and brought about by the presence of visitors.
- You could try preventing this by shutting your cat away before your guests arrive, or you could talk to your vet about trying a course of a mild tranquillising drug to see what effect it has.

MY CAT IS OFTEN SICK IN THE LIVING ROOM, ESPECIALLY WHEN I HAVE GUESTS. WHY IS THIS?

The first cat show ever recorded was at an English fair in 1598, but serious cat showing began nearly 300 years later, with a large show in 1871 at the Crystal Palace in London for British Shorthairs and Persians. In 1895 the first major American cat show was held in Madison Square Garden in New York. British shows are still run along the same lines as the very early shows, with cats judged in pens in private. In the United States,

10 Showing

however, the cats are judged on a table in full view of the public. In the United Kingdom, the body governing cat showing is the Governing Council of the Cat Fancy. Setting a breed standard and then judging individual cats against it is the essence of cat showing. The standard describes the 'perfect' cat for each recognized breed, and points are scored out of a hundred. Marks will be awarded for features such as:

- Shape and colour of eyes
- Type and shape of ears
- Type and shape of tail
- Body conformation
- Texture and colour of coat
- Shape and type of head
- General condition.

There are several good reasons for showing cats. Pedigree cat breeders need to compare their cat's bloodlines with others, to see how well their breeding programme is progressing. The kittens from a show champion queen will attract the highest prices, and the services of a champion stud tom-cat will be in demand. But there are other reasons for showing. People enjoy the opportunity to meet like-minded people, to admire other cats, to buy cat products, and to chat about cats. The important thing is to remember that it is for enjoyment.

why show your cat?

How to prepare your cat to enter the competitive world of the cat show.

CAN ANY CAT BE SHOWN?

- Yes. Many shows welcome mixed-breed as well as pedigree cats. Here, general condition and presentation score most strongly, since there is no breed standard for a more formal comparison.

- If you want to enter your pedigree cat in a show, you must be able to prove its breeding by supplying a pedigree certificate. Your breeder should have supplied this information when you acquired your cat.

HOW DO I KNOW IF MY CAT WOULD TAKE TO SHOWING?

- The only way to find out is to try it. Some cats really seem to enjoy being the centre of attention, whereas others look as if they are hating every moment of it.

- If your cat does not seem to be happy about being taken to a cat show, don't try to make the cat do something it does not want to do.

- Showing is fun only if both you and your cat enjoy it, and it is very unlikely that a cat cowering at the back of a pen (especially one that tries to scratch the judge) is going to win a prize.

HOW SOON CAN I SHOW MY KITTEN?

- You have a much greater chance of success in showing a cat if you get it used to the experience from an early age. Check before you enter, but most shows will accept kittens from four months of age.
- These young entrants normally go into a special kitten class, because a cat of this age will not have developed its final adult conformation and so cannot be judged fairly against mature cats.

IS IT TRUE THAT JUDGES ARE BIASED IN FAVOUR OF PARTICULAR CATS?

- In some countries, the cats are judged anonymously, with only numbers of the pens to identify the cats. This obviously helps to prevent any bias, as judges are only human (well, most of them are).
- The whole idea of having a breed standard is so that cats can be compared to an ideal and then scored objectively, but ultimately personal preferences will always have some influence. Some judges may favour a particular feature, such as a more elongated head shape in a Siamese cat.
- If you enjoyed the experience of showing your cat, but you didn't win a prize on that particular day with that particular judge, don't despair. It's a good idea to enter the cat under a few different judges to gain a wider consensus of its worth as a show cat.

Seal'point Ragdoll.

Blue point Siamese.

Seal point Himalayan.

Lilac point Siamese.

- These characteristics are fairly minor hereditary problems which are common in the breed, but not considered acceptable from a showing point of view.
- Legends grew up about these features of the original Siamese, which were imported from Siam (now Thailand) in the late 19th century.
- According to one legend, the royal princesses relied on their cats to look after their rings; these were kept on the cats' tails, and the kinks developed to stop them from falling off.

SOME OF MY SIAMESE CATS HAVE KINKS ON THEIR TAILS AND SQUINTS. IS THIS SERIOUS?

Seal point Siamese.

Blue tabby point Siamese.

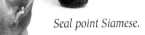
Red tabby point Siamese.

WHAT DO SHOW JUDGES LOOK FOR IN A SIAMESE CAT?

- A good show specimen should have a strong contrast between a light-coloured body and relatively dark points.
- Siamese-coloured cats (and this includes breeds such as Himalayans, which are longhairs with contrasting points) are unusual in that the colour of the points depends upon the body temperature difference between the extremities, which will be cooler and thus grow dark hair, and the trunk, which is warmer and thus grows light hair.
- If hair is clipped off the body, the skin will be cooler because it does not have its usual insulation, so the hair will grow back a darker colour.
- Similarly, if a foot is bandaged for any length of time, the resulting increase in skin temperature will make the hair grow a lighter colour.
- Siamese cat owners who show their cats often prefer to keep them in outdoor runs, because the cooler conditions will encourage a greater contrast between the points.

- You should find that a local show will welcome a newcomer and give useful advice and assistance to you and your cat.
- There are several cat magazines that advertise dates and venues for cat shows. Look out for a selection at your newsagent's or at your vet's.
- Cat clubs will also have newsletters listing shows that are relevant to your particular breed.
- You need to apply to the Show Secretary (the Entry Clerk in the United States) for an entry form, and you will then receive a slip confirming the details that will appear in the show catalogue.

HOW CAN I FIND OUT WHERE THERE IS A SHOW?

WILL I WIN MONEY FOR SHOWING MY CATS?

- If you plan to get rich from cat showing, think again. You have to pay to enter a class, and generally all you will win is a certificate, a rosette and the satisfaction of owning a top-class specimen.
- Of course, if you are interested in breeding, winning at a show will enhance the value of your breeding stock and their offspring.

preparation & procedure

How to prepare yourself and your cat for a show.

- First of all, from an early age accustom your cat to the routine that it will experience at shows.
- Get it used to being penned, to travelling in a cat carrier and to being handled by as wide a range of people as possible. If you own a longhaired breed, it is vital to start a regular grooming regimen from the outset.
- In the few weeks before a show, you will need to make sure your cat is in tip-top condition. A premium-quality diet should be fed at all times, and the annual vaccinations will need to be up-to-date and recorded as such on your vaccination certificate.
- The day before the show the cat should be groomed very thoroughly; make sure that the ears, eyes and claws are clean, and as an extra precaution, treat for fleas, unless it has been done recently.

I AM SHOWING MY CAT FOR THE FIRST TIME. WHAT EQUIPMENT DO I NEED TO TAKE TO THE SHOW?

- You should take the following:
- Cat carrier
- Litter tray—preferably white, so as to be as inconspicuous as possible
- Cat litter
- Vaccination certificate
- Show documentation
- Grooming implements, including a toothbrush
- Blanket—again, preferably white, and, of course, clean
- Water bottle and bowl
- Catfood and feeding bowl
- Disinfectant with which to sanitise the benching cage before putting your cat inside.

- It is common for longhaired cats to be bathed a few days before a show, particularly if the cat is supposed to be white but thinks otherwise.
- Most organisations do not permit the use of artificial coat-colouring agents, so talcum powder should either not be used at all or be brushed out thoroughly before the show.
- You have more of a chance of being able to bathe your cat easily if you start doing it regularly from a young age. Use a shampoo designed for frequent use on cats.
- Details of how to bathe your cat are in the grooming section.

SHOULD A CAT BE BATHED FOR A SHOW?

- Whenever many cats are brought together under one roof, there is an increased risk of infection.
- It is important that your cat be up to date with its vaccinations against all the major diseases, and many shows will ask you to produce your vaccination certificates.
- Pens are designed so that there are solid barriers between them and a good space for the aisle down the middle, which makes the spread of disease unlikely while cats are in their pens.
- Judges and stewards should disinfect their hands after handling one cat and before handling the next, and the inspection tables should also be thoroughly cleaned between cats.
- You should avoid handling other cats at the show, however cuddly they may look, or you could also unwittingly spread infection.

IS THERE MUCH DANGER OF INFECTION AT SHOWS?

- In some countries it is compulsory for every cat to receive a veterinary examination before entry to a show
- Particular emphasis is placed upon checking for infectious problems, such as ringworm, fleas, ear mites, or cat flu. A check is also made to ensure that the cat is not suffering from any common hereditary problems, such as cryptorchidism (undescended testicles) in the case of a male, or a hernia.
- This procedure is not generally carried out in the United States, where owners are relied upon to bring only healthy cats to a show, and any cat showing signs of disease would be asked to leave at once.

WHAT IS 'VETTING IN'?

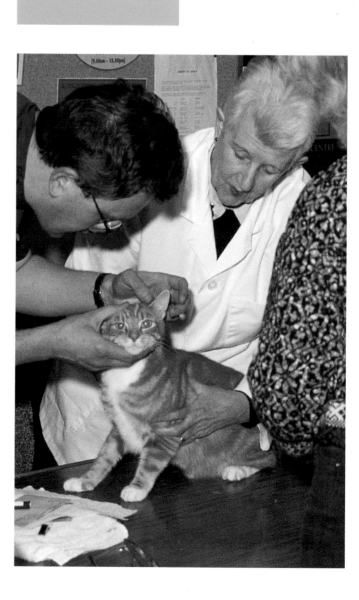

nervous competitors

How to reasssure your nervous cat.

MY CAT THROWS UP IN THE CAR ON THE WAY TO CAT SHOWS AND NEVER WINS BECAUSE HE GETS ALL DIRTY!

MY CAT IS ALWAYS NERVOUS WHEN BEING JUDGED. WHAT CAN I DO?

- This is less likely to happen if you accustom your cat to travelling from an early age. Avoid feeding your cat overnight or before setting out in the morning.
- You could get some travel sickness tablets from your vet, but you might find they make your cat look a bit bleary-eyed when being shown.
- Lots of very short journeys are the best way to get your cat used to travelling.

- This is another problem that can be avoided by starting early. Get your cat used to being penned and being handled.
- Your cat may feel more relaxed in front of the judges if you wear a white coat around the house, as the judges and stewards usually wear white coats when handling the cats.
- You could even try a mild herbal tranquilliser—skullcap and valerian—which may relax your cat without causing any sedation.
- If, after all your efforts, your cat is still not enjoying the experience, just give up.

index

acknowledgements

With many thanks to my beautiful wife Liz, and my children Emma and Oliver, for their patience when I have been attending to my word processor rather than them. Also my four cats, Clawdius, Cattius, Sculley and Mulder for doing their utmost to distract me from my work.
Bradley Viner

Quarto would like to thank and acknowledge the following for providing pictures used in the book:

Paul Forrester © Quarto: 23, 24(br), 25, 26(t), 30, 31(bl), 32, 33(r),34, 35(t, br & bl), 38(tl), 40 (tr), 46, 54(t), 55, 61(b), 68(b),69, 70, 71, 72, 73, 75, 76(tr), 77(b), 79, 84(br), 87, 98, 103, 104, 105, 107, 109, 111(t), 113(t & c), 119, 150, 151, 152, 153, 154, 156, and 157.

Bradley Viner: 38(bl), 53(tl), 85(t), 86(r), 91, 93(r).

All other pictures are the copyright of Jane Burton.

A special thanks to Crucial Books, London.